Freedom From Self-Sabotage

The Intelligent Reader's Guide To Success and Self-Fulfillment

Peter Michaelson

Prospect Books

Freedom From Self-Sabotage
Copyright 1999 by Peter Michaelson

All Rights Reserved. No part of this book may be reproduced or transmitted in any form or by any means without the written permission of the Publisher, except for inclusions of brief quotations in a review.

Library of Congress Catalog Card Number: 97-068491

Publisher's Cataloging in Publication Data
Michaelson, Peter
Freedom From Self-Sabotage: The Intelligent Reader's Guide to Success and Self-Fulfillment.
Bibliography: p
1. Self-Actualization (psychology) 2. Personal Growth
3. Applied Psychology 4. Self-Esteem

ISBN 1-882631-29-3

Design and Composition by John Cole GRAPHIC DESIGNER
Manufactured in the United States of America

First Edition April, 1999

Prospect Books
2912 Calle Derecha, Santa Fe, NM 87505
www.QuestForSelf.com

To all those individuals who seek
inner freedom and wholeness

Author's Note

The names and identifying details in the case histories in this book have been changed to protect confidentiality. Anyone with a history of emotional disorders should consult a mental-health professional before doing the exercises in this book.

Table of Contents

CHAPTER 1

The Secret World of Self-Sabotage *1*

CHAPTER *2*

*Why It Is Hard to Act in Our
Best Interests* *26*

CHAPTER 3

Transcending Our Self-Image *48*

CHAPTER 4

The Nature of Passivity *69*

CHAPTER 5

Victims of Ourselves *90*

CHAPTER 6

Sabotage in the Workplace *111*

CHAPTER 7

Mastering Inner Dynamics *136*

CHAPTER 8

Elements of Social Unrest *160*

CHAPTER 9

Freedom From Self-Sabotage *187*

Solutions and Exercises *198*

Notes *212*

Bibliography *213*

CHAPTER 1

The Secret World of Self-Sabotage

Just about every one of us has a story of woe, a personal drama of being defeated by our enemies, our friends, our parents, our situations in life, and, most agonizingly, by ourselves. We suspect that behind our defeat and our behavioral and emotional disruptions is some invisible saboteur. Until now we haven't been able to expose or apprehend this culprit.

This sabotaging aspect can be the primary cause of our addictions, compulsions, obsessions and phobias. It is a major ingredient in depression, low self-esteem, lack of purpose, and loss of spirit and heart. It seems to be the fuel for an inner combustion chamber that pumps out negative emotions such as anger, greed, envy, jealousy, loneliness, apathy, and the wish for revenge.

There are thousands of variations on self-sabotage. Here are just a few examples of how it has affected some people I have known:

* An attractive and intelligent woman chooses a man who she clearly sees has a drinking problem. Soon she finds herself feeling neglected and bitterly disappointed.

* A young professional has everything in place to prosper with his career. But he sits around in uncertainty and doubt, all his potential and talent going to waste.

* A housewife charges $7,000 on her credit card and gambles away all her savings at a casino. Her husband finds out and wants a divorce.

* A businessman's tennis game is solid and superb when he plays socially with his friends. But when he steps out to play in a tournament, all his skills desert him.

* An overweight woman loses sixty pounds in a heroic effort to look better and protect her health. Three months later, she's put ninety pounds back on.

* A man with a lovely wife and three bright children can't resist risking all in his dalliances with other women.

When under the influence of self-sabotage, people can be defeating themselves on several fronts at once. For example, a man's tendency to resist a controlling boss by being late to work and late with his assignments is hurting his career, at the same time that his marriage is being undermined by his desire to control and restrict his wife.

Often self-sabotage involves the predicament of seeing one's life become dissatisfying or miserable for no apparent reason. We just can't figure out what is happening. Things are obviously going badly, and we feel we would be willing to do almost anything to rectify our situation. But nothing that we try works. We just keep sinking deeper into the mire.

Self-sabotage has been called the enemy within, the shadow, and the inner saboteur. It has been referred to in clinical manuals as Self-Defeating Personality Disorder. It comes in many guises, stalking us in the form of self-denial, self-doubt, self-disapproval, and self-condemnation. At its worst, it constitutes not just self-defeat but self-destruction and self-hatred. It refers to a mysterious configuration that hides inside us and toils against our best interest. If we don't succeed in identifying and owning this sinister part, we can never be free.

I show in this book the configuration of this secret part of us and what we can do to liberate ourselves from its invisible shackles. This book illustrates self-sabotage on a personal level and provides numerous exercises for freeing ourselves from it. It also shows how, as individuals coming together in a collective, we subvert ourselves as a society.

This book teaches how and why we have been blind to our self-sabotage. Readers are privy to "the Big Secret" about our human nature. You will learn why this knowledge has not been assimilated by the public, and why even mental health professionals aren't conversant with it.

Perhaps our biggest obstacle to personal growth and self-fulfillment is our resistance to seeing through the defenses we have erected to hide the truth of our secret collusion in self-defeat and suffering. Our elaborate system of defenses is designed to thwart and repel any facts or knowledge that contradict what we want to believe about ourselves and the world. In a way, we are more interested in security and self-protection than the truth about our lives.

So this book penetrates into our defenses. It exposes the unconscious patterns that imprison us in cycles of frustration and futility. This is *bop*, not pop, psychology. It bops you on the head with evidence of your unconscious collusion in your misfortunes. So muster your courage as I expose your secret collaboration in your own self-defeat.

This book also presents insights into the art of feeling fully alive, for living at the highest levels, and for recognizing your true essence as a being of light and love. To achieve that, we need to overcome our separation from ourselves and our readiness to identify with a false sense of who and what we are. To do this, we start by examining our negative, sabotaging elements.

When we don't know what is going on inside ourselves, we often blame others or circumstances for our frustration and failures. We proclaim our "psychic" innocence, perhaps blaming "toxic parents," or an inherent or genetic weakness in ourselves, an abnormality or chemical imbalance, or "the cold, cruel world."

Or we blame ourselves for laziness, or lack of personality, or selfishness, lack of will power, and so on, which only makes us feel more helpless, defective, and dispirited. Often we slip into self-pity, proclaiming, "What's the use, it's hopeless—I'd be better off dead."

Scores of competing theories and ideas profess to know how we can best live. In the marketplace, you can choose from stacks of psychology books offering hundreds of variations—each earnestly endorsed—on the requirements for growth and positive change. Ask all the experts how to eliminate self-sabotage—they include personality researchers, behaviorists, gestaltists, developmentalists, primal theorists, psychoanalysts, psychiatrists, cognitivists, psycholinguists, neuroscientists, dynamic psychotherapists, and maybe your clergyman and family doctor—and you will get enough different answers to overwhelm the new supercomputer Pacific Blue.

Many people, including experts in psychology, believe that our emotional reactions and self-destructive behaviors are mainly the consequence of childhood mistreatment or the provocation of social injustices. Our culture still embraces the view of 18th-Century French philosopher Jean-Jacques Rousseau who said that humans are basically good, and only do bad things because of negative influences acting upon us from outside. I am going to show that, yes, while we are intrinsically good, we are nonetheless sabotaged by negative forces with a life of their own acting on us from *inside.*

Many of us still believe, as did the 17th-Century English philosopher John Locke, that the mind at birth is a "white paper, void of all characters, without any ideas," which acquires its operating capacity exclusively through experience. This view ignores the primary psychological endowments with which we enter the world—natural aggression, libido, and egocentricity. Soon after birth, our natural aggression becomes aroused by what are taken as affronts to our being, and this aggression is eventually turned into self-aggression. This happens because the powerful egocentricity, or intense self-centeredness, with which we enter the world causes us to be highly subjective and to misperceive reality in a way that generates feelings of being deprived, refused, controlled, rejected, and so on.

Simplistic views of our human nature have been blended into a psychological hash and dished out as fast food of the psyche in most of the country's mental-health facilities. This bland, processed knowledge consists of behavioral advice, positive thinking, cheerleading platitudes, and rational reinforcement. Since this diluted knowledge doesn't get to the heart of the matter, it is just a matter of time before we are passed on to the pharmaceutical industry for the anti-depressants and mood stabilizers that we are willing to ingest because nothing else has worked.

Popular jargon tells us we can be happier by *doing* such things as being nice to people so they will be nice to us. Or we are told, "Appreciate what you have, look how lucky you are." When we are trying to sort out a dispute in our lives, we might be told something to the effect: "Don't be passive! Don't put up with that nonsense! Don't let them do that to you!" Or a generic favorite for almost any ailment, "Think positive! Don't think negative, just think positive!"

Positive thinking has long been touted as a psychological antidote, so if it worked we would see a lot more happy people coasting through life. Throwing positive affirmations at self-sabotaging programming is like trying to kill a dragon with darts. Core questions have to be addressed: why is the negative there in the first place? Why is it so difficult to do what is in our best interest? Why don't we exercise more, eat better, stay focused, worry less, remain positive, keep friends, save money, hold on to love, and achieve more with our creativity and skills?

The problem of self-sabotage hinges on a formidable configuration in the psyche, what I call *emotional attachments*.

These attachments are a result of unresolved conflicts from childhood that are ultimately acted out in our relationship with ourselves. They arise out of the subjective impressions we take on from childhood of being deprived, refused, controlled, criticized, rejected, and so on. What traditional psychology fails to recognize is *our secret, emotional investment in continuing to experience, and even to indulge in, feelings associated with these repressed emotional memories of childhood.* Hence, the term emotional or secret *attachments.*

My belief in the existence of these attachments is based on my clinical experiences with hundreds of individuals as well as on the discoveries and writings of Edmund Bergler, M.D., a psychoanalyst who died in New York City in 1962 and whose work is described in some detail in Chapter 7.

Here is how such attachments affect us. A man who felt that, as a child, he wasn't loved by his mother will say he wants love in his life but will continue to be attached emotionally to the feeling of being *un*loved. Unable then to love himself, he is under the influence of an unconscious compulsion to act out his self-rejection and to expect to be unloved by the women in his life, all the while defending against these feelings by claiming that he is an innocent victim of their coldness.

As another example, a woman who felt controlled and dominated by her father when she was a child will choose either a man who dominates her or a man who she can dominate. Either way, control and domination remain emotional themes in her life. She interprets encounters with others in terms of control, even when control is in reality not an issue or is not the intention of the other person. On the surface, she claims to hate the feeling of being controlled and protests against it, all the while secretly thwarting and oppressing the expression of her highest good.

Emotional attachments have a life of their own and can be difficult to expose and understand. They reside in the psyche, hidden from sight like bugs or quirks in a computer system. Though we have all the ingredients to be happy and successful, these unconscious anomalies can thoroughly mess up our lives.

What exactly is an emotional attachment? It is an unconscious psychological configuration that compels us to interpret events or situations from a negative perspective. It is the tendency we have to feel that we are being deprived, refused, controlled, dominated, criticized, rejected, abandoned, betrayed, and so on, even when the actual events or situations to which we are exposed do not warrant in themselves such reactions. Unconsciously, we misinterpret situations in such a way as to rekindle these negative feelings and to embellish them, just as we experienced them in childhood.

Above all, an emotional attachment is a secret investment in the continuance of a particular negative experience. Through our defenses, we do not want to see how strongly we remain invested in experiencing these feelings and how we recreate and recycle them against ourselves.

Our evolution is marked by the struggle to overcome emotional reactions and acquire enhanced rationality. Any student of history knows how our ancestors have been steeped in superstition, hallucinatory states of mind, unwarranted fearfulness, magical thinking, self-destruction, hatred, violence, and war. Even the most prominent, cultured, or educated among us are mired in variations of negativity that arise out of our mysterious unconscious mind to disturb our lives in a thousand different ways.

Overcoming self-sabotage involves making conscious what was unconscious. This book reveals the ways that self-sabotage lurks in the unconscious and strikes at us like an invisible virus. Though we have the knowledge, the real problem is our resistance to assimilating it. This knowledge threatens our self-image. It disturbs us even as it sets us free. We avoid, deny, or fear knowledge that is powerful and liberating because of what it requires of us. As a psychotherapist who practices this method, I am in the position of telling people what they hate to hear. Fortunately, like the painless dentist, I have my means to make it quite palatable.

Nevertheless, as I expose this secret collusion in self-defeat, some readers will feel shame and humiliation as they consider, as many of my clients have said, that "this is really sick." It is an experience that combines disbelief, shock, sadness, and horror to see the extent of your own participation in self-defeat. This is a normal reaction to having your self-image challenged (if not demolished) and to seeing the influence of this unconscious antagonistic agenda. Sometimes we avoid assimilating this knowledge when we read or hear it by "spacing out," or slipping into a kind of pseudo-ignorance, or we become incensed and indignantly deny that this could be an aspect of us, proclaiming the absence of scientific proof.

If we can push through this resistance, the rewards are considerable. The healthy individual, free from self-condemnation, is able to live in the here and now, with a sense of having come home to himself. He or she becomes less self-centered, more compassionate, feels fulfilled in the process of learning and growing, and is aligned with activities that promote the well-being of all. A great deal of psychic energy that previously kept unconscious material repressed and defenses in place is now freed up for creative and imaginative pursuits.

For this to happen, we want to see how our emotions have a sophisticated "rationality" all their own that disrupts our well-being, thwarts our attempts at inner growth, and often rides roughshod over our cognitive abilities. A person's rational, conscious side is at a great disadvantage in subduing his emotional side *if the rational side is not well enough informed about the unconscious configurations it is dealing with.*

In other words, the emotional (or unconscious or irrational) side is much more powerful an influence than we realize, and it manages through the various defenses to hide from our awareness the nature and extent of the inner sabotage. Indeed, as unpleasant as it is to accept, we are dealing with a formidable foe, a tyranny of the unconscious so well defended that most of us, mental-health professionals included, have not been able to recognize its existence, let alone its structure.

It is an axiom of psychology that the greater the truth, the more we resist it—*for emotional reasons.* British playwright George Bernard Shaw, who was awarded the 1925 Nobel Prize in Literature, wrote that the greatest truths first appear to us as blasphemies—in other words, we have adverse emotional reactions to them. To the citizens of the 16th Century, Copernicus blasphemed when he revealed that the world is not at the center of the universe. How did these people experience this revelation? If the world wasn't at the center, what did this say about them? They must have felt, "If we're not at the center, does that mean we're not as special as we think?"

This was a crushing blow to their ego, their self-image. It felt like being reduced, humiliated, even to the point of feeling insignificant and unworthy. We have a powerful aversion to seeing how we resonate with this feeling. Many a person, claiming to be offended and insulted by someone else's slight of him, has started wars and killed people to avoid recognizing that this is how he secretly regards himself.

To 19th-Century men and women, Charles Darwin blasphemed when he wrote that we descended from the ancestors of apes. Again, it is the feeling of having our self-image drastically demoted. Cultivated people in the mid-1800s, who took such pride in their intellect's creation of the Industrial Age, were not eager to be exposed as the descendants of apes. How dare this fellow Darwin spout such a horrid proposition! But soon Sigmund Freud followed Darwin to add insult to injury. He too jolted the foundations of self-image when his discoveries informed the world that we humans are not masters in our own house. Unconscious emotional factors, Freud wrote, determine many of our thoughts, feelings, and beliefs, stranding us in the backwoods of consciousness far from our potential.

Of the three revelations, I believe Freud's was the greatest blow to our pride. Even today, one hundred years after his first book was published, only a small minority have assimilated for their personal benefit his discoveries about the unconscious mind and the vital knowledge concerning transference, projection, displacement, repression, identification, narcissism, and self-aggression.

When we overlook these unconscious dynamics and configurations, we are guarding our precious illusion of being King or Queen of our own inner domain, not caring to recognize, let alone acquaint ourselves fully with, the black-garbed Minister of State standing in the wings.

The Art of Self-Responsibility

Self-sabotage is, in large measure, a result of our deficiency in the art of self-responsibility. We can't see the configuration of our self-sabotage until we are able, at a deeper level, to become responsible for our negative emotions and behaviors. This requires some explanation. The concept of self-responsibility described in this book is more advanced than the traditional sense of being responsible. The traditional sense involves respecting others, obeying laws, taking care of our health, and contributing to the well-being of family, community, and nation.

Of course, opportunities are boundless for improvement in this expression of responsibility. But to acquire the power to rout self-sabotage we need what advertisers call a new improved version of the product, and *self-responsibility*, as I describe it here, is just that. It requires that we learn to become responsible not only for our obvious daily duties and moral obligations *but for our negative emotions and self-defeating behaviors as well.*

In other words, we begin to see our own participation in producing anger, greed, fear, paranoia, hatred, and the lust for revenge. Blaming is no longer acceptable. The spotlight shifts from the actions or attitudes of others onto ourselves and how we are choosing (often unconsciously) to react negatively or in a self-defeating manner to challenging circumstances. We become able to see more clearly our own role in producing negative outcomes and reactions.

Here is an example of the kind of insight we need to acquire to avoid self-sabotage. Jessica, a client in her mid-thirties, was returning to the same university she had attended seventeen years earlier. Only eighteen at that time, she started using cocaine, drank heavily, and dropped out of classes before the end of her first semester. Now, almost twenty years later, Jessica wanted to get a Master's Degree in Business Administration and she felt considerable anxiety as she prepared to move to the city where the university was located. Despite having just successfully completed two years of community college, she kept asking, "Am I really graduate-school material? Or am I just fooling myself?" Jessica kept recalling her earlier experience and feeling doubt and shame as the details of that failed semester were replayed again and again in her mind. "I don't like the person I was back then," she said, "and I don't want to think about that time in my life. But I can't shake the feelings of guilt and shame. Maybe I should go to a university somewhere else or just forget about it altogether."

I told her, "This time you have a chance to make it different because you're going to expose and understand your sabotaging tendencies. You're dredging up these memories from years ago, and obsessing on that earlier experience, because those memories serve a secret purpose. Despite your best conscious intentions, you remain emotionally attached to feeling wrong about yourself. Emotionally, you're willing to take on feelings of self-doubt and self-criticism. Your unconscious is replaying those memories so you can continue to doubt yourself and even to berate yourself for allegedly being a failure. This inner consumption of self-doubt and self-criticism produces guilt, anxiety, and shame. It's your way of wrestling with yourself and blocking your advance. If you were to go on dredging up those old feelings and soaking up the criticism, you could indeed undermine your present efforts and sabotage yourself in the present.

"So every time you catch yourself dwelling on that failed experience from years ago, you can flash on the realization of what you're doing, how those painful memories are coming up because you are emotionally attached to self-doubt and self-criticism. The problem is not your performance of years ago but your secret determination in the present to use those memories to condemn yourself. The more clearly you see this inner game of self-negation and self-sabotage, the easier it becomes *not* to play it."

In another example, a middle-aged man I met was wandering from town to town, unable to settle down and establish roots in any one place. He was miserable and professed how much he wanted to establish new friendships and settle in one community. But he couldn't make a choice on where to stay. Whenever he thought about choosing a particular town, he began to generate reasons why the place was unsatisfactory.

In the one session I had with him, he told me stories of friends he had made in various locales who had proven to be disappointing. He felt he wasn't finding the kind of quality friends he expected or deserved. After he disclosed some of his childhood history, which was filled with the feeling that he and his father had been a disappointment to his mother, I felt I understood his self-sabotage.

I told him, "You can't make a choice of where to settle down because of your emotional attachment to disappointment. You experience again and again the feeling of being let down and disappointed by new friends and situations. You're convinced the problem is external, that this town or those people don't offer you enough, when the problem is your own emotional inclination to feel disappointed and dissatisfied in yourself. You remain entangled in that old feeling of disappointment you had in childhood and direct it now toward yourself. You're fated to recreate it and act it out in the various contexts of your life as long as this form of self-negation remains unconscious.

"In childhood you felt you were a disappointment to your mother. Now you've reversed the emotional conflict and you have become like your mother, disappointed in yourself, so that now you project this inner feeling of disappointment onto others. One way or the other—whether you feel you're the disappointment or that others are disappointing you—that feeling still haunts you."

This wasn't what he wanted to hear. "No, no," he said. "I know that's not it! It's either the fact that my new friends let me down, or it's something to do with my indecision, how I make poor choices in where to go." And thus he left, not to return, disappointed again by his latest encounter and confirming what the sages have always known, that the secret intent and major life choice of many people is to take their suffering to the grave.

A third example concerns President Bill Clinton who, as I write this, is awaiting trial in the U.S. Senate on two articles of impeachment. As the child of an alcoholic step-father and a mother who had several relationships with abusive, addictive men, young Clinton at times must have felt humiliated, reduced, helpless, powerless, and under the influence of a person who had dominion over him and his family. These are all elements that, when unresolved, produce self-sabotage.

Clinton's sexual acting-out had these elements of power and control over women, as well as humiliation of them. His self-sabotage was to bring humiliation and possible loss of power down upon himself. We are all capable of comparable acts of self-sabotage.

Clinton tells us now—"I betrayed your trust." His trust in others was broken long ago during the chaotic circumstances of his childhood. Since we do onto others what we felt was done to us, we can further see in Clinton's actions the pattern and the compulsion to repeat to our detriment what is unresolved from our past.

Clinton's self-defeat is a reflection of our own propensity to sabotage our highest good. It also foretells the self-defeat that can occur on a national level if we don't consciously acknowledge the meaning behind our personal and collective issues. A good purpose—that of learning more about ourselves—can come from this process of reflection and assessment going on in Washington. Our political leaders, most of them trained in the law, appear to place little if any value in the notion that the enhancement of our self-awareness is a vital process in our evolution as a nation. Such an appreciation might have kept President Clinton out of the tar-pit of infidelity. Congressmen favoring impeachment kept telling us, "Truth is the foundation of our legal system." Perhaps they would have been more compassionate if they understood that falsehood is the foundation of our (unconscious) defense system and that the biggest lies, even greater than Clinton's, are the ones we tell ourselves.

Liberation from self-sabotage requires an understanding of how we *co-create* the life we experience. We are not innocent victims suffering at the cruel hands of fate. Rather, we participate in the circumstances of our lives by giving consent, consciously or unconsciously, to most of the pleasure or the pain we experience. Self-responsibility enables us to see that our reactions to the inevitable stresses and challenges of life are a result of choices that we are making. It requires the courage to acknowledge that we may have an emotional investment in maintaining our negative emotions and beliefs. It also requires reflection upon the concept, long established in psychological literature but still fearfully denied, that much of our lives is run by an unconscious agenda that is more aligned with defeat than the promotion of our highest good.

Self-responsibility also requires us to consider our own passivity—how we may be allowing ourselves to be manipulated and controlled, how we may secretly look for oppressors to malign us or hold us back, how we may be indulging in unpleasant emotions, and ultimately how we are identified with a false sense of who we are rather than with our true self.

I used to be a classic injustice collector. I was determined *not* to see how I fed on alleged injustices and used them to account for my unhappiness. In my first career as a journalist, I was a pain in the neck for city editors and bureau chiefs. Like the typical disgruntled employee, I was convinced that my ill feelings toward my work and my supervisors were validated by external circumstances. I had emotional conflicts that I didn't understand and wasn't facing. I didn't want to see that I was the one with the problem. Looking back, I realize that my bosses were mostly fair and reasonable. Even if I'd had a tyrant for a boss and had worked in a grimy sweatshop, the healthy response would have been either to leave with grace and dignity or, if I chose to stay, to conduct myself in a positive manner, possibly looking for ways to reform the situation. No whiner or complainer, nor someone aligned with feelings of defeat and convictions of inadequacy, is likely to achieve work-place reform.

Nowhere is the unwillingness to take responsibility more evident than in couples relationships. When a husband and wife, or boyfriend and girlfriend, aren't getting along, each is more likely to focus on the flaws and deficiencies in the partner, *to blame* the partner, rather than to turn the spotlight on himself or herself.

In a relationship, each partner is reluctant to see his or her role in a deteriorating situation. The man's role may be, for instance, his sensitivity to the feeling that he is being controlled by his partner. Even if his wife were attempting to control him, his sensitivity to the feeling is nonetheless the result of a lingering emotional attachment from childhood experience. Unaware of this connection to his past, he blames and resists his partner for controlling him when, in fact, based on his emotional memories of being controlled in childhood, he invites control by holding himself back, persistently forgetting, procrastinating, being unable to speak out his needs or make a decision, even as he protests how much he hates feeling controlled.

We all want to blame our unhappiness on others. Or we blame the government, or the system, or our parents. Sometimes we blame ourselves, but invariably for the wrong reasons. For instance, we may say our problem is laziness or a lack of personality, when these are only symptoms. As we are blaming ourselves for the wrong reasons, the primary sabotage deep inside the psyche may be, in a typical situation, our emotional willingness to soak up feelings of being drained, depleted, and deprived.

Most times we want to feel that our suffering is a valid experience, just what any normal person would feel in our shoes. We go around looking for evidence that we are entitled to suffer, that we have no choice in the matter, while we try to enlist sympathizers to vouch for the severity of our plight. Before we realize what is happening, we have become chronic complainers, injustice collectors, and jailers of our own free spirit.

Self-responsibility means, on a personal level, that we learn to face our fears and to discover the true origins of our painful emotions and failures. For instance, if you are feeling shame after having been scolded by your boss, and torment yourself about it for hours and days, you are reacting like a child to his parents, dredging up old feelings of being rejected or being seen as flawed and unworthy that you are now applying to yourself. Feelings from childhood do indeed persist, and the more we fail to see our lingering attachment to them, meaning the manner in which we are prepared as adults to rekindle and repeat experiences of these feelings toward ourselves, the more they haunt us.

With self-responsibility, we learn we cannot expect anyone else to make us feel better. If we are stuck in a dead-end job or marriage, we can't blame anyone else. This doesn't mean others are innocent and exert no influence over us. But we are ultimately in charge of *how we react* to external situations. "Life is ten percent what you make it and ninety percent how you take it," the saying goes. Maturity is the growing willingness to be responsible for our behaviors, decisions, and feelings. We are no longer children whose parents answer for us; we answer for ourselves.

As an exercise in self-responsibility, make a list of all the things you feel you should do or would like to accomplish. Here is an example of how your list might look:

a) I should lose weight.
b) I need to exercise more.
c) I want to clean out the garage.
d) I would like to spend more time with the kids.
e) I should be more intimate with my spouse.
f) I want to change my career.
g) I shouldn't be so sensitive to others' comments.

When your list is done, note for each statement all your excuses for not doing what is on your list. Start each statement with, "I can't (exercise, change my career, stop smoking, etc.) because…" Compare your excuses with the following list of creative excuses for not doing what is in your best interest.

* *There isn't enough time.* This is a common excuse. Obviously, other things have more priority. Ask yourself, "Why are

these other things more important than what's on my list? Am I secretly using the excuse that other things are more important so that I can continue to be attached to feelings of being deprived of what I really want or so that I can have ammunition to criticize myself for not achieving my potential?"

* *There isn't enough money.* Some people make sure there isn't enough money by spending it frivolously. That way they ensure they won't have money for what's important. What we spend our money on reveals a lot about how we regard ourselves. Ask, "Am I using being short of funds as an excuse to feel deprived, both of money and of my goals for myself?"

* *It takes up too much energy and effort.* Yet for an activity we are enthused about, there is seldom a shortage of energy. Ask, "Am I secretly attached to feeling drained and depleted, for which feeling like (or being) a failure is just a symptom?"

* *I'll have to give up too much.* Sometimes we use the feeling of missing out on something potentially more interesting or pleasurable as a way to avoid doing what is best for us. Ask, "Am I so attached to feeling loss that even when I'm struggling for something valuable I experience the struggle as a loss and thereby can't proceed?"

* *I won't be able to pull it off.* This is the feeling that our effort will fail or not work, so why bother. This excuse is often effective because sometimes things don't work out. If we don't undertake something, then we do not have to deal with a sense of failure with respect to that endeavor. Ask, "Am I too tempted to remain mired in feelings of passivity, of being helpless and powerless, to proceed on my quest?"

* *I'm under too much stress already.* We tend to put things off until we feel better. Of course, that day never comes because tomorrow it will be even easier to use stress as an excuse.

* *I'm just looking for bliss and ecstasy.* This excuse common to substance abusers serves to conceal one's self-sabotage in the pretext that the futile activity has some redeeming value.

We use such rationalizations to hide the real truth about our self-sabotage. To find the true self-sabotage, go over your list again and for each statement answer, "I don't want to (exercise, change career, stop smoking, etc.) because…(elaborate as fully and truthfully as possible)." As an example, here is how one man assessed his underlying motives for continuing his heavy drinking: "Stopping drinking will mean submission to my wife and that will make her happy. She and others will control me. Drinking also keeps my emotions and negative feelings under wraps. When using alcohol, I don't feel as much distress or discomfort. And I won't have to see how much I hate myself. I know I'll fall apart if I can't have a drink."

As another example, someone who can't lose weight might say: "If I lose weight, I won't be able to say *no* to the opposite sex. I'll be rejected. I'll feel insubstantial, vulnerable. I will have to please others. I'll feel deprived. I won't know who I am if I lose weight."

When we look deeper into ourselves, we see that much of our resistance to doing what is in our best interest includes the following motives: 1) to hide our unpleasant feelings, 2) to hide passivity and feelings of being forced to submit to others and let them have their way with us, 3) to mask our dependency on others for validation, 4) to keep us from falling apart, since we don't know who we are without our self-defeating behaviors, 5) to validate our belief that we don't deserve good in our lives, 6) to provoke rejection from others, 7) to give us a good excuse to disapprove of ourselves, 8) to keep us from having to change, and 9) to help us to avoid seeing our investment in loss, deprivation, and disappointment.

Ask yourself, "What role does a certain substance, feeling, or activity play in my life right now?" Suppose you have the urge to binge on food that you know is not good for you. Ask yourself: "Am I putting on weight to act out an emotional attachment to rejection? Am I tempted to eat this food so that

I end up feeling more defective and inadequate, and so that I can berate myself for being fat and ugly? Am I determined not to experience intimacy and love, and is this how I ensure I won't get it? Am I emotionally attached to disapproval and even self-condemnation, so that eating this food becomes a set-up to condemn myself afterward for having eaten it?" The food won't be so appealing when you taste the self-sabotage in the ingredients.

Finally, compose a list of all the things you want. Here is an example of such a list: 1) I want to leave my spouse, 2) I want a loving, permanent relationship, 3) I want to help or serve others, 4) I want to be happy, 5) I want more friends, and so on. Now, say why you want each item on your list. What will these things give you that you don't already have? Keep asking why till you reach the final motive. Then for each statement, say, "I don't want...because..." Dig up all the reasons and emotions. Can you begin to see more clearly how you sabotage yourself? What will happen if you don't achieve what you want? What will happen if you *do* achieve what you want?

The Challenge of Accepting Responsibility

We all want to be absolved of responsibility for our failures and unhappiness. Why? To lessen anxiety, to neutralize the inner accusations that hold us accountable for failure or lack of progress in our lives. We all have an inner voice that assails us with accusations of our alleged wrongdoing or inadequacy. Typical are these allegations: "What's the matter with you? Why aren't you doing this right? You should be doing better. You're always messing up." It relieves an inner burden if we can say in our defense, "It's not my fault; it's those extenuating circumstances that make my life so hard."

In medieval Europe, before our modern age of anxiety and ambivalence, everyone knew his or her place. If you were a serf or a peasant, not much was expected of you. You went out and tilled the fields, and you let the religious authorities decide what you were supposed to believe, who you were, and what your value was. Life was simple. Your fate depended on your status at birth, your ancestry, your blood lines. It is much different in modern America. Here you can create a great destiny for yourself, no matter what your blood lines. Now your success depends on skill, on personality, on your emotional strength and your own resources. In America, the message is, "You can be whatever you want to be."

That's great, especially if you have a long string of credits and successes to your name. But suppose you are *not* succeeding as you think you should. Suppose you are doing badly, getting nowhere. Such a predicament can become very painful. The inner conscience now comes at us: "Why aren't you doing well? All those others are doing better than you. You must be inadequate and worthless!"

We want to say: "No, it's not my fault! I'm not responsible for my situation. Circumstances are too hard. I have the meanest boss in town. I had a bad childhood. My father drank too much."

Blaming others lets us off the hook. Indeed, this line of thought may relieve some inner anxiety. But it is still just excuses. And it doesn't cure our emotional problem—our negative attitudes and feelings toward ourselves. If we follow this line of thinking, we become keepers of a victim mentality—depressed, sour, cynical, and bitter. We may also become "dependees," holding onto all sorts of infantile perceptions and believing we are entitled to be taken care of.

Our determination to avoid self-responsibility can be seen especially in addictive personalities. Many of them want to believe their problem is caused by a chemical imbalance, or bad genes, or the "disease of addiction." In making this claim, they decline to see or take responsibility for their self-sabotage. This leaves them clinging to their identity as addicts and limited by it, even when they have become abstinent. They don't want to see that their addictive behaviors are emotionally based. Every addictive personality is loaded with dissatisfaction, anxiety, and emotional pain, and is mired in feeling helpless and ashamed. His addictive behavior is a symptom, not the cause, of these feelings. But he is loathe to face his self-condemnation because it challenges his character and his self-image. He takes such self-examination as criticism of himself, as indications of being defective and unworthy which is exactly how he feels about himself. He has a hard time being objective about himself because he feels any truth points at an inner corruption that deep down he (1) believes is the ultimate truth about himself and (2) is determined to hide or deny.

All of us try to hide from ourselves. So for all of us the process of acquiring self-responsibility raises our anxiety levels, at least temporarily. We may be afraid to make important life decisions. For instance, a person in a troubled marriage often wants his or her partner to make the choice whether or not to get a divorce. One man I counseled had been tormenting himself for months for having initiated a divorce. His unpleasant emotions had little to do with whether the choice was good or bad, and much to do with his unconscious willingness to go on beating himself up verbally because of his emotional attachment to feeling criticized (the feeling is the same whether felt as self-criticism or criticism from others.) In other words, his emotional readiness to feel criticized left him with a chronic sense of having made an unwise choice. He "buys into" the inner accusation of wrongdoing, or "takes a hit" on it, whether the accusations are valid or not, and thereby experiences doubt, guilt, and shame.

That is why many individuals in similar situations are relieved when someone else makes a decision for them. They want to be spared the emotional challenge of being responsible and thus avoid being punished by their own appetite for doubt and criticism. I was told by a married woman in her late thirties who was ambivalent about having a baby: "Oh, I wish I were a Catholic. The choice would be made for me. It would just happen or it wouldn't." She felt guilt-ridden as she criticized herself for not wanting a baby, thinking she was a selfish person. But her guilt stemmed from the fact she was identifying with her imagined baby being unwanted and unloved, feelings she harbored toward herself—remnants from her own childhood of feeling unwanted and unloved.

Growth and exploration always evoke anxiety. Pioneers and explorers faced irrational fears in discovering new horizons and acquiring new knowledge. Acquiring self-responsibility is a learning process and a dissolving of boundaries within ourselves. It means moving away from childish beliefs and feelings and into adult maturity and emotional independence. It also means seeing the hidden motives and secret intent in much of what we do.

Suppose you are a person who rarely feels satisfied with his career, friends, and relationships. You decide to become responsible for your discontent. You learn that your discontent is a product or symptom of your emotional attachment to a secret readiness to believe that you are going to be deprived, refused, or denied in some manner. You begin to see how convinced you have been that you will miss out and not get what you want or need. You observe yourself in the process of indulging in feelings that life isn't sustaining or supporting you, while you become aware of being willing to see other people getting more than you. You recognize the chronic feeling: "Whatever I get, it's never enough." You see how you deny yourself, your feelings and needs, and realize that your overeating, drinking too much, overspending, miserliness, and so on are attempts to use food and money to fill your inner emptiness or emotional void. That void is the chasm-like space we all must cross over as we break through our self-hatred and self-negation and move toward loving acceptance of ourselves as we are.

Developing self-responsibility is so liberating because it leads us away from thinking that circumstances and insensitive people are the causes of our failures and unhappiness. That thinking had been making us dependent on the behavior of others to feel good about ourselves. It takes fortitude and resolve to move into self-responsibility, just as this process develops inner strength and character.

The self-responsible, self-regulating person is not without doubts or guilt. But he is not stymied by such emotions. He trusts his feelings, his instincts, for who he is, what he does, and what he may accomplish. He knows his own mind, makes his own decisions, stands up for his values, and expresses himself without fear of disapproval or rejection.

He becomes a detached observer of life. This doesn't mean, of course, that he is withdrawn and cold. It means he no longer personalizes situations or the behaviors of others. He is more patient, less frustrated and angry. He doesn't fight against life, nor does he drift aimlessly. He takes in the experiences of life, including the hardships, with trust and gratitude. He sees not from self-centeredness but with an acceptance of things as they happen, knowing what he stands for and where to make his stand.

Consequently, he is able to deal responsibly and creatively with the challenges in his career and relationships. He is able to be intimate and express his true feelings when appropriate. Self-reproach and guilt are gradually replaced by the development of his creative capacities and the ability to live by his own inner voice. He has learned to discern when that inner voice is true and when it is distorted by doubt, reproach, guilt, shame, and regret. He is motivated by creative impulses, integrity, purpose, competence, humor, and compassion. His life is balanced and stimulating, his work enjoyable, creative, and productive.

On a social level, self-responsibility produces more people who are aligned with the common good. People function at a higher level and life is richer for all because each is more interested in what he can do for others. There is less paranoia and violence, more interest in long-range planning and the well-being of future generations. A new spirit of cooperation and common purpose replaces the widespread emotional problems of isolation, narcissism, and alienation, the price we pay for our separation from our true self.

This integration brings inner balance, an end to the inner war of opposites between good and bad, right and wrong, pleasure and pain. The individual is grounded in his self-understanding; he takes care of himself and acts in his own best interests, while remaining sensitive to the feelings and experiences of others. Now he is steeped in character, meaning he is aligned with what is wise and he acts accordingly.

In attaining this, we give up nothing except our inner conflicts and our suffering. That alone produces resistance in those who have to wean themselves from an emotional attachment to conflict, who can't position themselves in the world without their internal miseries and external enemies.

CHAPTER 2

Why It's Hard To Act in Our Best Interests

In this chapter, we plunge deep into the unconscious to learn the essential elements of self-sabotage. It is scary at this depth, like submerging into one of those six-mile-deep oceanic canyons to come face to face with spiked aquatic creatures as ghastly as we imagine our worst inner demons.

Our submergible for this plunge is not a reinforced-steel sphere but the story of one woman's experience, presented in the opening pages of this chapter as a little monograph titled "The Emotional Secrets of Melinda." Our heroine Melinda descends into the dark depths of her psyche to find the source of her unhappiness and self-sabotage. Courageously, she brings to the surface of her awareness emotional material that had been repressed and forgotten. Now, exposed on the surface, the material remains challenging for her to absorb because it flies in the face of her logic and common sense.

The first chapter of "The Emotional Secrets of Melinda" consists of what is elementary and obvious about Melinda, an interior decorator who happens to be a compulsive shopper. The second chapter tells us more about Melinda and the nature of her sabotage, while the third chapter exposes the core issues, or the profound truths at the heart of Melinda's self-sabotage. The fourth and last chapter represents the process whereby Melinda overcomes the sabotage and finds peace within herself.

Chapter One. Melinda is excellent at her work and makes a

decent income from it. However, her personal life is completely unsatisfactory. She is depressed and irritable, and often feels she isn't adequate or good enough as a person. She subjects herself to a constant barrage of self-criticism, feels drained and exhausted at work, and resents having to focus on her husband's needs.

Larry, her husband, is a businessman who puts his work first. He is often critical of Melinda, appears to take her for granted, and is reluctant to spend money on her although he is generous with his relatives and full of compliments for them.

Melinda often broods, *He doesn't give to me, pay attention to me, or show that he cares. In fact, no one listens to me. My feelings are ignored or dismissed as insignificant. I don't get a loving, caring response from Larry or from others.*

Chapter Two. On weekends, Melinda spends her leisure time shopping. She buys on impulse and often doesn't wear what she buys. Her closets are stuffed with clothing. She has more than fifty pairs of shoes and insists on buying from the most expensive shops. "Whenever I feel depressed, I go shopping," Melinda explains. "I feel better for a while after I've purchased a couple of new outfits." She becomes angry and defensive when her husband brings up the problem of her spending and attempts to curtail it. The self-sabotage is evident: she is $25,000 in debt on her credit cards and her spending problem is threatening the marriage as well as the couple's financial situation. Nonetheless, Melinda feels unable to alter her behavior.

Chapter Three. Now we come to the underlying problem. Melinda is convinced Larry doesn't care about her or her personal interests. She complains, "My whole life revolves around him—his decisions, his wants, and his needs. I'm just a little servant girl." Melinda contends that she doesn't get her needs met by a husband who, she claims, is self-absorbed and self-preoccupied. However, despite her conscious wish to be appreciated and loved, she remains entangled in her self-depreciation and self-neglect.

Unconsciously, she is acting out with Larry her attachment to being up against someone who (like her father) is self-absorbed and indifferent to her feelings and even her existence. In other words, based on her childhood experience, she expects this indifferent response from Larry and she is emotionally invested in continuing to experience it. Her compulsive shopping is a symptom of this conflict as well as a defense against it. The defense, played out unconsciously, goes like this: *It's not true that I seek to feel ignored and abandoned emotionally. It's not true that I ignore myself and abandon myself. Can't you see how much I hate that feeling! And look, he really is stingy with his affection and money. Since he won't give to me, I'll give to myself and make him pay.*

So she attempts to deny or cover up her emotional indulgence in self-neglect by giving to herself in an externalized, indulgent manner.

The feeling of neglect was familiar: Melinda's brooding, silent father never gave her much emotional support or validation. By overspending, she is trying to counter her unresolved feeling of being a victim of others who are self-absorbed and don't recognize and acknowledge her. Meanwhile, she gave plenty of time and energy to her father's needs and interests, just as she does now with her husband (going along with his interests in books, movies, restaurants, and hobbies). But she resents much of it. *See how much I put out for others. And they still don't notice me or respond. Therefore I deserve to get all I want when I want it. Since they're insensitive to me, I'll be insensitive to them.*

The more Melinda spends, the more she invites her husband to treat her coldly and to resent her insensitivity to his wishes. Now Melinda feels even more neglected by him as he reacts with resentment toward her. Typically, self-sabotage intensifies the negative emotions we hate the most.

Chapter 4. Melinda begins to acquire new insight into how she is attached emotionally to feelings of being refused, neglected, and abandoned emotionally. She realizes her secret agenda is to deny and neglect herself. All the while she has been using blame, denial, passive-aggressive reactions, and other protests and defenses to cover up her self-oppression. She sees this more clearly by doing the following exercise:

  * What do you feel you are missing out on in your life? Do you feel gypped or cheated in any way? Do you frequently find yourself mired in these feelings?

  * Where in your life do you expect *not* to get your needs met (for instance, in your relationships or career)? List your expectations with respect to loss and deprivation.

  * Make an inventory of recurring disappointments in all areas of your life. How are you disappointed in yourself? Is this not evidence of an emotional attachment to this feeling?

  * List the parental messages you received about fun, success, pleasure, or getting for yourself.

  * List your parents' patterns of self-denial. How did they deny themselves? Compare with your own patterns of self-denial.

Melinda sees that her self-sabotage is being expressed through symptoms such as her anger, apathy, depression, irritability, boredom, gloom, and out-of-control spending. She is aware these symptoms spring out of her emotional attachments to feeling deprived and neglected. (Were these attachments to remain unconscious, they could easily become more intense and disruptive as she gets older.) Larry's shortcomings mirror that part of her that is insensitive and neglectful of her feelings and needs. In reacting to him, she is acting out her own negative, self-denying part.

Instead of challenging him directly about her feelings, she has been reacting passive-aggressively, in a way that thwarts him as she thwarts herself, while sabotaging their relationship. As she works on her feelings toward herself, she sees her situation differently; she is no longer triggered by Larry and ceases to "act out" with him. Because of this shift in her, Larry changes too and ceases to oppose her.

As her understanding deepens, she observes that she slips less frequently back into old patterns. She is now moving forward out of those bumpy ruts, on to smoother terrain where her life takes on new satisfaction and pleasure. In the months and years to come, as she sees more fully her part in reactivating negative emotions from her childhood and dumping them on herself, her compulsive shopping ceases completely, along with her dissatisfaction and feelings of neglect, and she establishes a new relationship with herself full of respect and appreciation.

So Melinda's is one version of the game we all play with ourselves. Do you see through her example how our negative attachments and feelings toward ourselves keep us locked into old, self-defeating patterns? In the unconscious, we are willing to endure and exacerbate the very thing we say we hate the most. We are determined to experience and to maintain in our lives feelings of neglect, deprival, abandonment, and rejection, even as we are aware how much that hurts us.

Freedom from our emotional attachments and thus from self-sabotage hinges on our ability to recognize our secret investment in three categories of primary emotions—deprivation, control, and rejection. Our entanglements in these emotions have their origins in early childhood.

The first category of primary emotions to which we are unconsciously attached consists of the following aspects of deprivation: Expecting loss, feeling starved and going without, feeling deprived of what you really want, missing out, never having enough, never feeling satisfied, drained ("They take everything from me; I get nothing"), feeling ignored and neglected, not allowed to have fun, refused, held up, denied, can't have for oneself, disappointed, peeping (watching others get while you go without; watching others get away with things); feeling mistreated, gypped, ripped off, and taken advantage of; seeing others excel and feeling less.

Many of us sense an emotional emptiness at the core of our being. We may feel lonely or discontented, or have a strong sense of deficiency or loss. We feel trapped in these feelings and don't see a way out.

To compensate for the dissatisfaction or emptiness, we try to substitute with something that feels like getting. As babies, our first sense of receiving was oral (getting food or other satisfaction through the mouth). Thus it feels to us that taking in something or getting something—whether material goods, alcohol, drugs, food, recognition, money, or sex—is the easiest way to resolve our inner emptiness. Overindulgence in these areas only makes matters worse because it intensifies the inner emptiness rather than alleviates it.

Few of us have entertained the notion that we may crave the experience of craving. Emotionally, the craving itself is the payoff. In other words, the craving exists *as a defense that covers up how much we are emotionally attached to the feeling of being without the thing we crave.* In this unconscious defense, we are saying, "I'm not looking to feel deprived or refused. Look how much I want to have this! My desire for it proves how much I really want it!" This is an effective defense because it convinces us we really do want what in fact we are attached to *not* having.

Our earliest sense of deprivation was oral—when the milk didn't always arrive on time for instant gratification, we hollered and cried in protest. We began to experience that the world outside wasn't providing us enough of what we wanted or needed. As adults, we are burdened with symptoms of this underlying emotional attachment that can include feelings of being dissatisfied, selfish, depressed, greedy, impatient, entitled, and so on. With such feelings, we act out with hundreds of variations of self-sabotage.

In essence, we are emotionally invested in the feeling that something is missing or is being withheld from us. What is missing is our connection to and love for ourselves. Rather than expose this estrangement, we try to fill up the missing portion of ourselves through material acquisition and substances. But it is like pouring water into a leaky bucket; desire by its nature remains unfulfilled. The more we reject ourselves, the more we feel that something is missing. The more we remain dissatisfied, the more likely we are to lose control of our behaviors and emotions in the futile quest to compensate or cope. The chances increase that we will become addictive, compulsive, obsessive, or phobic.

Let us look at an example. Susan feels left out by her friends who are apparently too busy to go out with her on Saturday night. She settles into the feeling that her whole life consists of watching others have fun while she sits home by herself. She sinks into this feeling as if it were quicksand. Feeling sorry for herself, she binges on cake and wine. Why? Her overindulgence in food and drink feels like a remedy for the anguish of feeling abandoned and unloved. But take away the emotional factor—her indulgence in these feelings—and she would have no anguish and hence no compulsion to binge on substances.

Think for a moment how difficult it is to feel gratitude for what we have, or how challenging it is to feel good about ourselves. Think of how pervasive are the feelings of being let down by life, disappointed in ourselves, in others, in our jobs and relationships. Doesn't this chronic condition indicate the likelihood that some part of us is invested emotionally in the expectation and feeling of being deprived, refused, and drained?

For many people, there is never enough money, food, recognition, sex, or power. Behind their cravings lurk the secret hunger for an empty breast, unrelenting poverty, eternal emptiness, and a feeling of emotional starvation. "Not true," we may say in protest, in defense, "I'm not secretly aligned with feeling deprived and empty. Look how much I want to get! Look how eager I am to get in any way I can! My crime is really wanting too much!" We would much prefer to plead guilty to being greedy or selfish and have that recognized as the problem, rather than consider the problem's true source—our secret longing for an empty breast .

This corresponds with my inner experience. Chronic dissatisfaction, resulting from my readiness to feel that something was missing in my life, was one of my favorite forms of suffering. Daily I watch that part of me that likes to jump on center stage like a circus barker and recite his litany of life's missing ingredients. I can observe this loud-mouth in me and even listen to him without nodding in agreement as I used to. But still he catches me napping and I start to dream about more money, more recognition, more love. "You're being a beggar," I tell myself as I recognize my indulgence, an indulgence that has its roots in my ongoing dissatisfaction with myself.

Some psychologists say that we only need to cultivate a feeling of gratitude to overcome feelings of being deprived or refused. However, I contend that feelings of gratitude cannot be permanent and genuine unless we first come to terms with the starving beggar who lurks in our psyche, wanting only to feed on the feeling of what he is *not* getting. We need to become responsible for the myriad ways we starve ourselves of happiness, pleasure, and love.

The second category of primary emotions to which we are unconsciously attached and which instigate self-sabotage comprises variations on feeling controlled. These include feeling under the influence of something or someone, taken advantage of, used, beaten down, ripped off, conned, violated, lied to, persecuted, intimidated, trapped, forced to submit, pushed around, dominated, restricted, inhibited, restrained, held up, made to endure inappropriate behavior, imposed upon, obligated, made to look bad, forced to pick up the burden or do it all oneself, required to see things their way, told what to do, overwhelmed, helpless, and consumed.

Many of us unconsciously set ourselves up to be controlled and dominated. As children, we spent years feeling controlled and under the influence of our parents. Consequently, many of us continue to have an unconscious affinity for feeling powerless and helpless in our lives. As adults, we are primed to recreate circumstances in which we again find ourselves being controlled, manipulated, and dominated—by bosses, spouses, friends, our children, the situations of our lives, the government, and our own impulses, desires, and addictions.

When we feel unable to regulate ourselves in whatever external situation, we feel taken over by something bigger than ourselves. In our passivity, we allow ourselves to be under the influence of something that dominates us. There is an unconscious willingness to remain in submission to this force, despite the suffering it causes. A frequent factor in alcoholism and drug addiction is our secret willingness to come under the influence of substances that we can feel are more powerful than our will to resist.

Often self-sabotage consists of our passive-aggressive reaction to feeling controlled. A young boy feels controlled by his mother. He feels he is told how to think and feel, how to behave, and even what to wear. Unconsciously, he feels a desperate need to express some sense of power to counter the terrible feelings of passivity and helplessness he experiences. He becomes anorexic and accomplishes this feeling of power by starving himself. Now it is his mother who is helpless to influence him. His anorexia is emotionally based. Though his resistance is unconscious, he has found a passive-aggressive way to rebel against the control of his mother, though at a great cost in self-sabotage.

In another example, a mother wants her daughter to lose

weight. The mother makes derogatory comments about her daughter's figure and tells her what foods to eat and not eat. The daughter rebels by putting on more weight. She does the opposite of what her mother wants in order to resist submitting to her mother's demands. Yet, regrettably, she now is unable to resist or moderate her own self-defeating rebellion.

All of us display passive behaviors at various times (again, this is a remnant of our infantile situation with our parents). Here are several more prominent passive behaviors and feelings that are forms of self-sabotage:

* going along with the agenda of others, agreeing with their perspectives, accepting their negative behaviors.

* sacrificing on an on-going basis your wants and needs; putting other people's feelings and needs before your own.

* rarely speaking up or expressing your feelings; letting people walk over you.

* feeling compelled to take blame and to explain or defend your behaviors or reactions.

* being suggestible; believing what others say; allowing others to make your decisions.

* enduring unhealthy or painful situations and not taking action to change your difficult circumstances.

* being in a state of perpetual confusion about what you want.

* procrastinating and being forgetful.

Having a difficult time self-regulating often indicates that an individual has unresolved conflicts from past parent-child power dynamics. A child depends on his parents to control his impulses and to place boundaries on his behavior. As he grows into adulthood, he must internalize these controls and acquire self-regulation, or else he needs outside sources to help with his regulation. Requiring outside sources, while at the same time resenting them, is a characteristic of a painful expression of self-sabotage, that of the "dependee."

Many of us avoid confronting our emotional issues in order to avoid feeling that we are submitting to the person (such as a parent, spouse, or boss) who is requesting or demanding reform from us. It feels as if we are being controlled when we allow someone else to help us or guide us. We may also feel that we will lose ourselves in the process, just as we felt as children when our parents towered over us with their expectations and demands.

The third category of primary emotions to which we are unconsciously attached and which instigate self-sabotage comprises variations of feeling rejected. These include feeling criticized, unloved, abandoned, betrayed, deserted; no longer important, not wanted, excluded, neglected, pushed aside, left out; looked down upon, put down, humiliated, insulted, criticized, judged harshly, not understood, not liked, hated, unfairly accused, disqualified, discounted, dismissed, not recognized or acknowledged, seen as incompetent, ignored, not supported, not validated, let down, disappointed, seen as worthless, condemned.

As children, it seemed that we were never loved enough, or in the right way, and that our siblings got more attention or validation. Since we are not objective as children, we can easily feel not loved enough and consequently have resistance to loving ourselves. As adults, we don't see how pervasive is our self-rejection and our expectation of feeling unloved.

One of the most common forms of sabotage is self-rejection. With the attachment to rejection, we often reject ourselves more harshly than even our worst enemy. We disapprove of ourselves for being imperfect and having flaws, even though being imperfect is entirely human. We also reject and berate ourselves for past mistakes. Sometimes there is so much self-defeat to remember, so much we can't forget, that it is easy to condemn ourselves and bemoan the cost of our foibles and folly. But often, foolish things were done because it couldn't have been any different given the insidious nature of self-sabotage.

If we felt our parents didn't value us, then we have a hard time valuing ourselves. We treat ourselves with the same negligence that we felt we received from our parents (we often compensate by boosting our narcissistic self-preoccupation). I believed that my parents reacted to me and my creative projects with indifference, that they took me for granted. As an adult, I transferred onto others the expectation that they would respond to my writing with the same indifference. I also felt that women would react to me with indifference. In fact, that is how I felt the universe responded to me—as if I didn't matter at all. So too, I responded with the same indifference to myself, to others, and to my health concerns and long-term well-being. Through it all, I maintained illusions of superiority, sometimes appearing to others as arrogant and aloof. At bottom was my emotional attachment to this unconscious wish: "I want people to overlook me and see me as nobody special."

To explain to ourselves why we are feeling unloved, we conclude that we are defective and unworthy. Consequently, it becomes difficult for us to act in our own best interests and expect others to truly care about us. Let us say you make a mistake at work and are called in by your supervisor to discuss the mistake. You take your supervisor's criticism personally, as a rejection of who you are and what you have accomplished. It is the old absolutes again—if I am not good, then I am bad. You feel ashamed, humiliated, and disapproved of (which was how you felt as a child whenever your actions or performance were questioned). That night you binge on ice cream or get drunk. The next day you beat yourself up for being "an irresponsible slob." You criticize yourself for overeating or drinking too much, which masks the real issue of your continuing indulgence in feeling rejected, criticized, and disapproved of.

Here are some frequent indications that reveal an emotional investment in self-rejection: 1) obsessing that others see you as ugly, stupid, foolish, or inadequate; 2) fearing you will be rejected for expressing how you really feel or think; 3) fixating on your alleged faults, or frequently reflecting on other people's alleged faults; 4) feeling offended when others disagree with you; 5) taking other people's behaviors and comments personally, as a rejection or belittling of you; 6) promiscuous behaviors; 7) a need to be perfect; 8) frequent bouts of jealousy or imagined betrayal; 9) overworking to prove yourself worthy; and 10) envying others, feeling inferior to their success or accomplishments.

I have witnessed many clients take the insights from therapy as criticism and beat themselves up with disapproval and self-rejection (recreating the non-acceptance they felt from their parents). This is why treatment methods or systems based on the "disease concept," the idea that genes or biochemistry cause addictions and other dysfunctional behaviors, are so eagerly embraced. The disease concept absolves us of blame: "They tell me it's a physical disease. Therefore, it's not my fault. I can't help being an alcoholic. I'm not so bad after all." This rationalization can ease anxiety and even assist in attaining abstinence. But it doesn't uncover or disturb the emotional attachments to such feelings as refusal, control, rejection, and criticism that are buried at the core of addictions. It doesn't cure our self-hatred and self-negation. Self-regulation won't flower from rationalizations or soothing consolations. It comes from taking full responsibility for our own collusion in self-defeat, in a manner which truly illuminates the battle within ourselves to squelch our highest good.

The Hidden Source of Negativity

Many people will scoff at the notion that we create the circumstances that maintain and reinforce these negative emotions. But don't such attachments, fueled by our self-negation, explain why we stay mired in negativity and patterns of self-sabotage, despite our best conscious efforts to escape? We are smart people. We think we know what is good for us and what isn't. So why aren't we happily pursuing a life of prosperity and fulfillment? We haven't been ready to see our inner saboteur in all his power and antagonistic design, just as in society we haven't been ready until the last several decades to begin to see and address the extent of emotional, physical, and sexual abuse in the family.

Okay, you say, maybe this is true. But how could people possibly become attached to negative emotions?

The condition can be traced to the extreme self-centeredness with which we are all born. All we know at birth is our own body and our sensations. In our mind, nothing exists outside of ourselves. This sense of "oneness" with reality leads the child to feel that everything that happens to him is what he has wished for. If a rattle appears in baby's hand, that is what baby wanted to happen. In his primitive consciousness, a baby deduces: "Everything that happens to me is what I want."

So how does an infant begin to explain unpleasant feelings of being refused and deprived? He is hungry but the breast isn't present. Mommy is running around taking care of other kids or putting supper on the table for the family. Baby doesn't care about her need to attend to others, nor does he understand the relativity of time. If it takes mommy five minutes to get to him, that is an eternity of being deprived as far as he is concerned.

The child forms the impression that *he himself* must have wished for the experience of *not getting* the breast or bottle. He must have wanted to feel refused and deprived: "It happens— therefore I wished it. Since it's what *I* wished for—therefore it's what *I* want." This emotional accommodation supports his illusion of "oneness," temporarily at least, before cold reality overthrows it in the coming years.

In this belief, he *libidinizes*, or "sugar-coats," the feeling of being refused, deprived, missing out: "Since it's happening, *I* must want the deprival or *not getting* to happen. Yes, this is what *I* want." However, in making this rationalization and protecting this belief in his powers, he pays a big price. He creates an emotional attachment to feeling refused, deprived, missing out (*category one* of the primary emotions mentioned earlier in this chapter). Later, from ages two to three, through toilet training and early socialization, he makes a similar accommodation with feeling controlled and becomes attached to the feelings of being controlled (*category two* of the primary emotions). From ages three to five, as he becomes more aware of mother and father as separate identities who have a relationship independent of himself, he becomes sensitive to feelings of being rejected and unloved (*category three* of the primary emotions).

As he grows up, he makes adjustments of course to accommodate the reality beyond himself. But his appetite for feeling deprived, refused, controlled, rejected, criticized, and otherwise victimized has been cultivated and may even increase in intensity into his old age.

Contributing to this problem is the natural aggression we are born with in order to survive. The child's frustration and anger may feel as substantial to him as they would feel for an adult. Yet, the child's musculature is too weak to expel this substantial aggression into the environment. Despite the child's temper tantrums, his hitting and flailing, he cannot direct all the aggression outward. It is thus *introjected*, turned inward toward himself. As the child grows, the aggression begins to flow back at him as self-aggression. As an adult, his self-aggression largely takes the form of self-doubt, self-criticism, self-condemnation, and self-hatred. The more insightful we are, the more we neutralize or deflect the untrue and harsh allegations of our self-aggression. When we are insufficiently aware, we absorb the self-aggression and come to believe that the consequential bad feelings about ourselves are justified by our faults and weaknesses. When we are attached to feelings of criticism and disapproval, we have resistance to seeing self-aggression for what it is—misplaced aggression in the form of random, unwarranted attacks upon our essence.

The closer we move to our true self, the more we replace self-aggression with feelings toward ourselves of compassion, support, understanding, and love.

We have difficulty seeing our self-aggression for what it is. Instead, we are simply aware of its consequences—anxiety, loneliness, guilt, fear, a sense of alienation, self-doubt, self-rejection, and self-hatred. Often we turn around the self-aggression and project it outward, becoming critical, judgmental, and hateful toward others, even friends and family members, with whom we act out the negative relationship we are having with ourselves. Our self-aggression can be most easily observed when we realize how critical and disapproving we are of ourselves, sometimes simply for being human.

Through all of this we remain blind to our attachments, even to the most painful one, our attachment to the feeling of our own self-aggression. Our defenses, enlisted to cover up our attachments, prevent us from seeing how we soak up the self-aggression. We must remember that, in this unconscious reckoning, the prime directive requires that our collusion in suffering and self-sabotage be kept secret, especially from ourselves.

What are some of the defenses behind which we hide crucial self-understanding? Several of the principle ones are described below.

1) *Blaming others and blaming life.* Even as we secretly cultivate feelings of being victimized and hold ourselves back because of our own unconscious attachments, we look outward beyond ourselves to pin our misery on someone or something. This defense includes rationalizations and excuses and is explained in numerous contexts throughout the book.

2) *Identification.* If your parents judged and criticized your performance, you will likely be a judge and critic of other people's

performances, even as you continue to be sensitive to feeling judged yourself. You will do to others what you experienced your parents doing to you, and you will be convinced that your negative feeling toward the recipient of your criticism is validated by his or her behaviors and attitudes. The defense goes like this: "I'm not looking to feel criticized—I'm the one who is doing the criticizing." However, as you are blaming or being critical of someone, you are indulging indirectly in your own attachment to feelings of criticism through identification with how you imagine the other feels in being criticized.

In other words, to avoid feeling ourselves passive to a critical partner (a feeling formerly experienced at the hands of a parent), we reverse it and become the critic (just like our parent) and subject others as well as ourselves to the treatment we received.

3) *Displacement.* You take the emotional reaction from one situation and displace it onto another. A writer feels that his wife spends too much money on clothes and groceries. He grumbles at her, but doesn't communicate directly about his underlying feelings. However, he begins to experience writer's block. He feels tired even before he sits at his computer. Words that once tumbled profusely from his mind and heart now dribble out like a slow oil leak. Because he is secretly indulging in feeling drained by his wife, the feeling has spread to his writing. He faces the prospect his income will drop if his writing deteriorates and output declines, leaving him to feel even more drained in supporting his wife.

4) *Projection.* You accuse others of the faults you are guilty of yourself. For example, you say to someone (or think it to yourself), "You're not trustworthy" or "You're lazy." This is the gist of accusations that are coming at you from your own inner conscience. You take the accusations and cast them into the environment. As the accuser who casts the first stone, you are blinded by your self-righteousness, your protestation of innocence.

In the unconscious, we hear, "You're just like that lazy fellow, aren't you? You're worthless and untrustworthy yourself." We reply in defense, "No, I'm not like him! Look, I hate what he represents! I want nothing to do with someone like that."

As another example, a woman is passive with her boyfriend, allowing him to influence her unduly and dictate how she manages her life. Meanwhile, she gets angry at her mother who she says is too easy-going with the family dog, allowing the animal to mess in the house. The daughter is projecting her own passivity with her boyfriend onto her mother, hating what she sees in her mother that she denies in herself. By projecting in this way, she covers up her attachment to feeling controlled and pushed around.

In another example, you are feeling dissatisfied with your marriage, convinced that your partner's shortcomings are causing you to miss out on romance and love. But you are projecting your own shortcomings onto your partner.

To test whether you are using this defense, think of the major flaws you see in those closest to you and reflect on whether those flaws also apply to you.

5) *Transference.* This is the unconscious compulsion to experience current events and relationships in a manner that revives emotional hurts from the past. For example, you might consistently feel that you don't get anything of value from your spouse when the main problem is your transference of this expectation onto him or her based on feelings from your childhood that mother, or father, or both, never gave you anything of value. You suppress these feelings, decline to talk about them with your spouse, and transfer them onto life in general, feeling the world has become a cold, rocky coastline with no shelter or comfort. Meanwhile, your marriage is being swept up on the rocks.

As you can see, a person who is unaware of this and other defenses will fail to see his contribution to the problem and will be in a weak position to become more responsible in order to regulate his feelings and behaviors. He is prone to react to the perceived injustices through anger, withholding, lack of cooperation, hostility, and by initiating or provoking the breakup of the relationship.

6) *Claim to power.* This is the defense of blaming ourselves for the wrong reasons. It is explained in Chapter 3.

7) *Assorted Tricks.* Other common defenses include reducing to absurdity a comment or truth which challenges us emotionally; finding contradictions, even when they are inconsequential, to denigrate what we hear; using authority figures to contradict what we don't want to hear; evading an issue by minimizing our mistakes, failures, or crimes; slandering or denigrating those who challenge us emotionally; changing the subject; the *magic gesture* through which we give to others what we secretly feel they or the world withholds from us (example in Chapter 3); *cause-and-effect thinking* (examples in Chapter 4).

8) *Resistance.* Our resistance is an element in all the above defenses, but it is worth mentioning separately to isolate it and help us to recognize it. Much of our resistance is completely unconscious. A man gets tired, for instance, and falls asleep just before he is scheduled to go for couples counseling with his wife. An unemployed man who is feeling sorry for himself delays calling about a free career-counseling opportunity. A woman is continually twenty minutes late for her therapy sessions.

Resistance includes our pride, stubbornness, refusal to see through our defenses, refusal to consider what may be true about ourselves, and refusal to learn or give value to the importance of insight. It also includes our difficulty in feeling good about ourselves and our accomplishments and talents.

I once counseled a man in his sixties who had made millions of dollars in business but who was estranged from his two sons. His stubborn need for control had driven them away. I wanted to show him that he had put his sons in a no-win situation by his manner of relating to them, and that his self-centeredness and need for control were by-products of how he had experienced life with his own father. But his resistance was monumental; he wouldn't consider this possibility and he became defensive. He was determined to go on believing in the unworthiness of his sons. To do otherwise felt to him like an invalidation of his whole life. His self-image got in the way; to acknowledge his misunderstandings was to shatter that image.

Such is our resistance to seeing our collusion in pain and defeat that even those mental-health professionals who see the extent of our self-defeat are reluctant to lay it on the couch. One psychiatrist, when asked why he didn't confront his patients with this knowledge, said, "It adds insult to injury to tell someone who is suffering, 'You're bringing this on yourself.'"

It sounds as if he is saying, "We must be careful not to offend anyone with allegations of his self-defeat. It's better to suffer than to face up to such unpleasant facts." Sure, the truth offends our pride and thus it is uncomfortable. But facing the truth of our unwitting participation in self-sabotage is like lancing an infection: the initial hurt is soon replaced by healing.

Many psychological systems don't acknowledge our substantial resistance to inner progress. On the political and social stage we have seen powerful opposition line up against reformers when they tried to end slavery, institute women's vote, enhance civil rights, and protect the environment. This opposition can be vicious and cruel, yet it is only a reflection of the inner determination we all have to block our own progress, our own self-actualization. The reactionaries, those most threatened by forward progress, represent a part in all of us that prefers to stay with what is old and familiar, even if it is not working adequately anymore. Most of us only know ourselves through our identity, the accumulation of our experiences, beliefs, and sensations that comprises our limited or false self. It feels as if this is us and it is all we have. Painful and restricted as this limited identity may be, maintaining it can feel preferable to facing the unknown and going through the void in what is a death-and-rebirth process of transformation.

We want to think and see in new ways. It is a bit like learning to see the 3D computer-generated illusions produced in the *Magic Eye* books. We can start by understanding that the most effective way to become positive, to learn self-responsibility and eliminate self-sabotage, is to see clearly into the negative. The whole inner balance of power shifts in our favor when we see into the self-defeating relationship we have with ourselves that maintains our negative beliefs and feelings. Then good feelings and wise choices come of their own accord.

What could be more of a conundrum, a paradox, a challenge for human ingenuity, and a prank on our pride than a condition in which we consciously aspire to win, to get, to be free and loved, while beneath our awareness we are emotionally invested in losing, not getting, and in feeling oppressed and unloved? Erich Fromm, writing about human nature in his book *The Heart of Man,* said we must arrive at the conclusion "that the nature or essence of man is not a specific *substance,* like good or evil, but a *contradiction* which is rooted in the very conditions of human existence."[1.]

Another problem in assimilating knowledge such as this is our unwillingness to make an effort to understand that which appears too complex. We want so much for things to be simple. Understanding our attachment to negative emotions requires some mental gymnastics, as well as assimilation of the knowledge on a feeling level. It is a process that compares with the challenge of learning a new language.

For many of us, acquiring new knowledge is seen as too much effort, involving too much deprivation, and the giving up of something pleasurable or needed. Consequently, the need for change is resisted and our emotional issues denied or minimized.

We are also reluctant to face ourselves because doing so brings up childhood feelings of fear, guilt, shame, humiliation, abandonment, self-loathing, and self-hatred. As children lacking objectivity, we took so personally every little implication of our wrongdoing. We felt our parents only loved us when we were good and obedient. So we greet our feelings and flaws with the same reservations. Children often lie because they are afraid the truth will reveal them to be bad. Truth is equated with shame and punishment. Adults have the same problem. We don't want to see the truth because, in this childish, irrational way, it brings up old feelings of shame, guilt, and the conviction of our badness.

The defects we feel about ourselves do not correspond with objective reality. Nevertheless, the emotional conviction of being defective or unworthy often takes precedence over any external accomplishments that indicate the contrary. We need to expose our deep unconscious readiness to believe the worst about ourselves and to expect that others will also affirm these misguided beliefs locked in our emotional structure.

CHAPTER 3

Transcending Our Self-Image

Many of us spend our lives preoccupied with self-image. We obsess about our appearance and performance, enhance our attributes out of all proportion, and agonize that others might see our weakness. We do things mindful of our impression on others, and we confuse who we are with a fantasy image of what we want others to see in us.

In this chapter, I show how this identification with self-image, which is a byproduct of our underlying egotism or self-centeredness, influences our lives and is a factor in self-sabotage. Through our self-image, we are convinced we are in charge of our thoughts, feelings, and beliefs, an illusion we strive to maintain. But this self-deception is dangerous, for it renders us blind to self-sabotage whose influence over us depends on the degree of secrecy in which it operates.

Investment in self-image involves an emotional preoccupation with oneself. It is a limited identity, a perspective from which nothing matters so much as one's own feelings, interpretations, pleasures, and reactions. Under its spell, whatever one possesses or achieves is employed for self-aggrandizement to bolster and maintain the image. From this mentality, the long-range consequences of our actions and the common good are not factored in with our personal schemes and dreams.

Why can't we just be who we really are? Why does self-image even exist? We are, in a sense, beings who are lost to ourselves, who know ourselves through a false impression of who we are. We identified with our parents' actions, traits, beliefs, feelings, attributes, as well as the prevailing notions of reality, resulting in the formation of a false self at the expense of our true being.

From childhood, we are encouraged to rely on outside influences to define and orient ourselves rather than inner experience and intuitive feelings. In our culture, parents, teachers, and others tell us who and what we are, and we fail to see that in doing so they are projecting on to us their own personal notions of who and what they are. We are defined through testing, IQ, grades, obedience, performance, personality, appearance, status, and so forth, rather than for our essence and our experience.

We may know intellectually that we are good and accomplished, but emotionally we can feel otherwise. We are sensitive to any implication that we don't measure up. Deep inside we resonate with doubts about ourselves and whether we do measure up. We feel a nothingness inside that we run from. We expect to be judged, evaluated, and found wanting, because that describes our relationship to ourselves. Thus our actions are governed by narcissistic preoccupation that compensates for our sense of being inadequate or bad and having no substance or value.

Who we truly are is not only hidden from us by our emotional attachments but also by false impressions that have been draped on us like rags. We use self-deception to keep this system intact because we don't know who we are without the emotional definitions provided for us by parents and society.

The typical person's sense of reality, however distorted or painful it may be, gives him his orientation in the world and can feel as precious as life itself. We are stricken with fear when our self-image is threatened because it feels that, should our image evaporate, we will lose our identity, our conviction of who we are, and thus cease to exist.

When our self-image is challenged, it feels as if we are being exposed and condemned in a way that brings up shame. As children, it would have been considered shameful conduct on our part for us to have challenged our parents' view of reality. We avoid introspection—seeing into ourselves—because our first visual impressions concerning ourselves rested on how we felt our parents regarded us. We all harbor impressions that our parents saw us in some negative light and thus to see into ourselves is to see what is shameful and bad. Experiencing our sexuality and our feelings was forbidden. Thus, our curiosity shifted to non-sexual objects or conditions in the external world, while the unconscious memory of the prohibition against "self-examination" remained in place.

When we are aware of the nature of self-image and our investment in it, our self-centeredness begins to ebb. Our investment in self-image is toxic when it is mostly unconscious. Then we are missing the deeper awareness that keeps our egotism in check, and a shallow, subjective counsel rules our actions and pursuits. We become oblivious to the impact of our actions on others and on the environment. The more we try to feel substantial and worthy to cover up the insecurity of not knowing our true selves, the more we elevate the false self, feel it to be sacrosanct, and are thus willing to do almost anything to gratify it.

When we dwell on our desires, complaints, and shallow self-interest, we are thinking about *me,* about what *I* want, what *I'm* not getting, how *I'm* being held back or somehow oppressed. We imagine everyone is focused on *me*—how *I* look, how wonderful *I* am, or how flawed and inadequate *I* am. We are preoccupied with *my* concerns, perspectives, opinions and desires.

Investment in self-image causes us to feel separate from one another, blocked from compassion and love, and deprived of a sense of higher purpose and direction. In being preoccupied with self-image, we are focused on immediate gratification, and how the world deprives us, validates us, or opposes us. Our center of gravity revolves around what we are getting or not getting. We feel frustrated because the world doesn't conform to how we think it should be.

We believe, as author Daniel Quinn put it, that the world was made for man and man was made to rule and subjugate it. This mentality will continue to prevail and exalt our illusion of power over creation until some apocalyptic disaster humbles us or until enough of us recognize the ways we distort our sense of self and our place on earth.

The process of dissolving self-image enables us to feel with renewed certainty that we are part of something much greater than our own selves. We begin to see how we can be in a partnership (rather than a conflict) with our own unconscious forces, once we acquire the humbling but liberating appreciation of the psychic agenda that influences our lives so acutely as it protects our false sense of self.

Being self-centered doesn't necessarily carry a moral connotation. It doesn't mean we are "bad." This egotism or self-centeredness of ours isn't so much an indication of a lack of character as a lack of consciousness. Self-centeredness is an aspect of our human nature, a legacy of the powerful egocentric mentality with which we come into the world. Humankind has needed it for self-preservation, for survival in an environment that was hostile and indifferent. As Erich Fromm has written, "In man the instinctive apparatus has lost most of its efficacy—hence narcissism assumes a very necessary biological function."[1]

Self-centeredness can take the form of arrogance, vanity, greed, and snobbery, all the while masked by its opposite—pseudo-generosity. For example, the emotional and behavioral condition known as codependency appears on the surface to be based on one's concern for others. Codependents can appear virtuous and altruistic as they try to rescue and rehabilitate others.

In their toleration of inappropriate or abusive behaviors, codependents are secretly motivated by an unconscious need to return again and again to feelings of being deprived, refused, neglected, and disappointed, which is what they feel when others don't respond to their overtures and also how they feel in their own relationship with themselves. Their defense or cover-up avows: "I am kind and generous. Look how much I give to others. If only everyone were as thoughtful and sensitive as me. If only others would treat me with the same kindness."

This defense is called a *magic gesture,* and one of its intents is to cover up an individual's secret indulgence in feeling deprived, rejected, or neglected. The magic gesture is intended to "prove" the person really wants to get love and validation by making the claim, "This is how *I* want to be treated. I treat these others in this nice way because that is how I expect to be treated myself." This individual believes this claim, and thus covers up his emotional attachment to feeling refused or neglected. Consciously he wants positive experiences of prosperity and love, but unconsciously he is under an inner mandate to live out the expectation of *not* getting them.

A self-centered intent of emotional caterers is to feel superior to the one being helped. That satisfaction in feeling superior derives from an emotional conviction of being inferior. Because of this underlying emotion, caterers identify with those who are floundering in low self-esteem. Because they are so desperate to feel a sense of value, they rescue others as a means to embellish their own self-worth ("Look at how important I am to that person"). But caterers deny the other person his need to take responsibility for himself. They "enable" the other person to live without facing himself. Until they get to the roots of their compulsion to experience themselves through others, they cannot help themselves or anyone else become mature and independent.

Shallow self-centeredness contributes to another defense,

what is called *cause-and-effect*. Under the influence of this kind of thinking, we believe we are *acted upon* by people, circumstances, and events rather than seeing that our reactions are our responsibility, that they are produced by our own emotional interpretations through our co-creative exchange with life. Although we are tempted to believe otherwise, we are not innocent victims being acted upon by others. A person might believe, for example, that his anger is justified by his friend's insensitive remark. He wants to believe his friend *caused* his anger, that his anger is the *effect* of his friend's action. But, in most instances, if his anger were analyzed, he would see that it is produced by his own unconscious willingness to feel offended or belittled. We need to see that we interact with others according to our own readiness to indulge in, or "get hit up with," condemning attitudes toward ourselves. We are co-creators with the world and each other of our experiences *and* how we interpret those experiences. When we are protecting self-image, however, we are reluctant to see more deeply into our own illusions and self-negation, and thus we don't see our own collusion in generating negative experiences. Since cause-and-effect thinking serves as a defense against seeing our collusion in generating negative reactions, breaking out of it creates the terrain for substantial inner reformation. (More on this in Chapter 4).

Another of the unconscious mind's ingenuous defenses is constructed around our self-centered orientation. It is called the *claim-to-power defense*, and unfortunately it is seldom recognized or exposed in traditional psychotherapy. As an example of it, an individual would put forward the following defense to cover up an attachment to the feeling of being deprived or *not getting*: "Not true I am passively attached to feeling deprived. The problem is, I don't deserve to get. I'm not good enough. I'm defective, flawed, and inadequate." In this defense, the individual maintains the illusion that, in being defective, he causes the deprivation to happen. This claim-to-power defense enables him to feel he has some power, some influence over what he is experiencing, rather than acknowledging his emotional attachment, in this case his passive willingness to soak up the feeling of being deprived. This defense requires that he plead guilty to some "lesser crime" such as being inadequate or a failure, rather than admit his fascination with loss.

So, in exchange for covering up his attachment to the feeling of *not getting,* he has to pay a price (his pound of flesh) in guilt, anxiety, and shame for the claim to power that the *not getting* happens because he is defective, flawed, and inadequate. In maintaining this defense, he accepts guilt and shame for allegedly being defective, and that impression of himself becomes a cornerstone of his identity and a major contributor to his low self-esteem. This claim to power is used in order to preserve his self-image and to be assured that, though he may be navigating like a drunken sailor, he is still in the pilot-house propped up against the wheel.

Strange though it seems, we would much rather see ourselves as defective than to own our vulnerability and our collusion in the misfortunes of our lives. To protect our false self and its claim to power, we choose (unconsciously) to remain in a state of ignorance, like a passive population that, while living under political tyranny, is convinced through propaganda to support press censorship.

One way to bypass the censors is to catch ourselves dwelling on the kind of impression we imagine we are making on others. Whenever we are preoccupied with how others see us, we create through our self-absorption more separation from ourselves. At such a moment, we recognize and evaluate others exclusively for what they may be thinking of us—good, bad, or neutral—or more precisely what we *imagine* they are thinking of us. And what we imagine they think about us is precisely how we feel about ourselves. We bounce our own inner condemnation off of others. Consequently, we swing back and forth between two types of reactions. One is a manic effort to look good in order to raise our estimation in the eyes of others as well as in our own eyes; the other is helplessness, irritation, fear, and depression because our idealized self-image is not being affirmed by others.

Consequently, we don't see others but rather "half-see" them, meaning that, emotionally, we see them looking back at us with what we believe they are thinking or feeling about us. We are certainly not appreciating them in their own right, which is the very neglect we complain about having experienced with our parents and others. Parents in their self-centeredness often take their children for granted or even feel (unconsciously) that their children are only extensions of themselves. Most parents see an image of what they believe their child is, an image that reflects their own feelings toward themselves. They don't appreciate the actual, unique, body-and-soul being who stands before them. A large percentage of the adults I see in therapy are still hurting emotionally from their childhood experience of not having been recognized, appreciated, and validated by their parents. These individuals now struggle to recognize, appreciate, and validate themselves.

What does a child feel when an adult looks at him but doesn't see him? As my memory serves me, it left me feeling empty, alone, and unimportant. I felt I had nothing of value to offer, that my existence didn't matter, and that I wasn't worth relating to. In this predicament, I could barely register with myself or feel positively toward myself because it was apparent to me from the way I felt I was seen that nothing in me was worth recognizing.

When we experience this, we become non-existent to ourselves and our inner world. All that is left for ourselves on which to build an identity (a false self) is the accumulation of impressions that we received. We react to others and to ourselves according to these impressions. The accumulation of impressions becomes our self-image.

This insensitivity to ourselves results in the insensitivity with which we deal with one another. It is one and the same: I regard you the way I regard myself, and I regard myself the way I feel you regard me. We overreact emotionally to the perceived insensitivity of others because it reflects our insensitivity toward ourselves, which is a consequence of our lingering attachment to the feeling of being treated with insensitivity as a child. As we did as children, we fixate on the negative implications of what is said or done, take to heart allegations of being defective or wrong, and feel offended, helpless, and defeated. If someone disagrees with our position or chooses a contrary path, we may feel rejected or betrayed, and assume his independent actions are intended to hurt us. Or we may feel that he is right and our position is therefore wrong. Thus we sabotage ourselves in hundreds of ways—including missing out on love, friendship, and other benefits—when our investment in self-image erects a wall around us. Behind this wall we buy into these subjective impressions, losing our objectivity.

In the process of inner liberation described in this book, escape from shallow self-centeredness involves the absorption or assimilation of this self-knowledge; at the same time we observe our entanglements in self-doubt, self-reproach, and self-condemnation. If we address our negative emotional reactions more effectively and understand more profoundly the self-negation that prompts them, our humanity can be refined and we can successfully manage the tumult and turmoil that rapid change and growth will continue to bring.

Ways Our Childishness Persists

Shallow self-centeredness is due partially to the lingering effect of the egocentricity with which we are all born. We come into the world with the psychological elements of aggression (needed to survive), libido, (the pleasure principle—a yearning for what feels good), and "oneness," the inability to separate ourselves from outer reality.

The infant experiences only his own body and sensations. For the infant, existence revolves around himself since he is not separate from it. In his mind, mommy and daddy, even objects, are just extensions of himself.

I explained in Chapter 2 how the child acquires negative emotional attachments. To state it again briefly, the child, who is unable to separate himself from outside reality, believes that whatever happens to him is what he wants. Thus "bad" things such as being deprived or refused when the food he wants is not instantly available *must also be what he wants.* Through this manner of interpreting his world, he integrates, "sugar-coats," or *libidinizes*—meaning becomes emotionally invested in—the feelings of being deprived and refused, resulting in an emotional attachment to these negative feelings.

The child believes that he is the sum of existence, that nothing exists apart from himself, and that everything that happens to him is what he has wished for. If mommy puts a rattle in his hand, in his mind that happened because he wanted it to happen. If mommy isn't present to provide instant gratification, he believes that too is what he has wished for, unpleasant though it may be. Growing up is a process of identifying oneself as separate from outer reality, resulting in the formation of a unique individuality. But this all-inclusive perspective nonetheless persists in all adults and develops into a shallow self-centeredness, in feelings of being powerful, and in the belief we cause things to happen.

The following list illustrates the degree to which irrational and self-centered perspectives of an infantile nature are maintained in the outlook of adults. We don't exhibit these various modes of childishness because we are inadequate or defective.

Rather, they indicate the level of our consciousness or the degree of our evolvement. The self-defeating aspects of our limited consciousness can definitely be remedied through higher learning.

1) *Immediate gratification with no effort.* A baby can't wait patiently for the prospect of good things happening in the future. An infant has no capacity to reflect on past or future. Like an animal, he lives solely in the *now.* All that matters (besides the management of his fears, aggression, and illusions) is libidinous satisfaction, or the lack of it, in the present moment. The infant never appreciates what he gets because he feels it is all self-given, that he caused it to happen.

Adults, too, love to fly now and pay later. That is one reason there is so much debt. We want immediate results, fast foods, magic pills, and instant solutions. Many aren't willing to strive for years with required dedication toward achievement and mastery; that feels too much like deprival in the present. Even the economy, many observers say, rests on infantile impatience, on next week's paycheck or next quarter's earnings reports, rather than on a foundation of long-term planning and development.

2) *Being at the center.* When a baby cries persistently in a hushed movie theater, the public's annoyance is for the adults minding the baby and not the baby himself. We know the baby isn't responsible because he has no concept of disturbing others. We are annoyed at the self-centeredness of the adults who are being inconsiderate of the impact on others of their child's crying.

Among the millions of people who don't appreciate how their actions affect others are bad drivers, careless workers, insensitive bosses, and indiscriminate polluters. They aren't interested in being accountable for their actions. They don't have a feeling for the consequences of what they do because they are so preoccupied with their own narrow self-interest.

How *they* feel or what *they* get out of a situation is all that matters. Such self-absorption can be so profound that the effect on others is not only discounted but it is not even imagined. As an extreme example, some criminals are only able to show remorse when, through rehabilitation programs, they come for the first time into an emotional awareness of the terrible consequences of their crimes.

3) *Having the power.* Children believe they cause things to happen. When a husband and wife divorce, their child believes he has done something to bring it about. If mommy is depressed, her child believes he is responsible and that, magically, he should be able to fix her. (This can throw him into a profound sense of helplessness as he struggles with his misguided sense of responsibility.)

A man believes, "If only they'd make me the boss, they'd see how good a job I'd do. They'd see how smart I am." A politician is convinced that if elected, he will transform the government or the state. Empowered through his investment in self-image, he convinces others, who then support him and later watch him flounder in the whirlpools of reality. Some adults believe their actions cause bad things to happen: "The earthquake happened because we sinned." Or they take total responsibility for the actions of others: "If I'd spoken up, the fight wouldn't have happened," or "She wouldn't have left me if I'd been nicer."

4) *Magical thinking.* In their egocentricity, children believe that they have a special relationship with the universe, that the sun comes out to make them happy, that the moon follows them on walks, and that it rains because they have been bad.

Many adults put their faith in good-luck charms and other forms of magical thinking. They might believe, "If I lose my job, that's a sign to move." They like to believe they can make their problems or weight go away with a pill. Often adults believe that things *should be* a certain way and they are offended that reality doesn't correspond to their wishes. A radio personality wrote a book titled, *The Way It Ought to Be,* in which he appears to be offended that things weren't the way he thought they should be. Abraham Maslow, a former president of the American Psychological Association, wrote that, "To be strong, a person must acquire…the ability to perceive physical reality as essentially indifferent to human wishes."[2.]

5) *Win-lose.* Children see the world as white and black, good and bad, win and lose. "If she gets, I lose. If Tommy's bad, I'm good. If I submit, mommy wins. If Sally doesn't say yes, she's not my friend." Children believe there is only one way to see things. They believe they see things the only right way. Or they may believe that mommy or daddy sees things the right way and they don't.

Adults say, "Americans are the best," or "If my team loses, I'll feel rotten." Or they think, "She's so beautiful and I'm ugly." Someone else's success means *my* failure. The Republicans feel they lose when the Democrats win, and vice-versa. Some of us are emotionally fixated on being right. If we are right, then we are not wrong and thus we are okay. Since our sense of value is based on being right rather than wrong, there is no room for middle ground or open-mindedness. It is hard to accept that both can be right, both can be good, when we are stuck in the childish way of seeing that it is either good *or* bad, right *or* wrong.

Adults are quick to judge and disapprove of others for seeing things "the wrong way." And if you see things the wrong way, you're bad. We are convinced that our way is the right way and that others are misguided. It is difficult for many adults to give the differing perspectives of others as much weight as their own beliefs.

6) *The only one who feels this way.* A child believes his experiences are unique, and that he is the only one who feels a certain way. If a child is enmeshed in feelings of rejection, it seems to him that he is the only one in the world who is suffering in this way. As children, we believe that no one else in the world

could know what is happening and how we feel. Often we feel misunderstood and alone.

As adults, we are often surprised to discover others feel the way we do. This is noticeable in psychotherapy groups where participants, especially those new to the process of revealing their deepest feelings, often say, "It's so comforting to know I'm not the only one who feels this way."

7) *This will never end.* That is the little child's feeling that a rainy day will never end. The infant has no sense of relativity, and so the feeling of something unpleasant, such as waiting for the breast or bottle, seems like eternity. The child descends into the feeling of being deprived and bursts into wails of anguish, while his suffering is interpreted emotionally as a permanent condition.

For adults, suffering over an emotional crisis such as a relationship breakup is especially severe when it feels as if the pain will never end and love won't ever come knocking again. Adults also lose the ability to save or wait for benefits in the future when they become preoccupied with missing out in the present.

8) *Never get enough.* Children resent sharing and are quick to feel deprived. If Susie's piece of pie is bigger, Billy feels deprived, even if his pie is not only delicious but also more than enough. A child can fixate on some treat that his parents are withholding. The more he feels refused, the more he wants it. All he has received in the past counts for nothing. Gratitude is fleeting or seldom experienced.

Adults hoard their wealth and benefits too. At the thought of giving or sharing, they become emotionally preoccupied with how much less they will have. Getting more feels like the way to happiness. Getting less produces anxiety and irrational fears. As more special interest groups spring up to protect their entitlements and benefits, the nation fragments into competing factions.

9) *Bold assertions without facts.* Children often believe they only have to say something for it to be true. It feels in their self-centeredness that their points of view require no substantiation. Youngsters believe their own lies because their assertions are so convincing even to themselves.

Adults also make bold statements without substantiation. A man says, "They're out to get me, I know it!" Or, "I know what's she doing behind my back!" Though he can provide no evidence, or flimsy evidence at best, he remains convinced that his statement is true. He "just knows." At other times adults maintain the belief that, "If I can't remember it, it didn't happen!" Some adults say, "My childhood has no bearing on the present," and because they have said it they believe it and close the book on the subject.

The Shattering Effect of Self-Preoccupation

Self-preoccupation is an inherent human aspect that we can moderate by observing and acknowledging it. Instead, however, we celebrate it through our worship of celebrities. We identify with the celebrity's importance and aspire to his state of being. As children, we all wanted to be special and to be treated as such. Now as we observe celebrities being treated as special, we swing emotionally between extremes, loving them and identifying with them to tweak old memories of our childish grandiosity and to cover up our resonance with feelings of being unrecognized and unimportant, and wanting to demote them because we feel inferior under the inner accusation that we are not as good as they are.

Society today is like a morality play gone awry. The play had been progressing well, with hero, heroine, villain, and other actors creating a unity of plot and purpose, portraying well the art of life, and mindful of the deeper meaning of events and circumstances. Suddenly one of the minor actors, a narcissist compelled by an accumulation of modern pressures to "liberate" himself from anonymity, steps out of character and, with bluff and bravado, takes over center stage to deliver a self-absorbed soliloquy about his feelings and goals while the audience and other actors look on in embarrassment.

No one is a minor actor in life unless he feels himself to be insignificant. An exemplary person may be satisfied playing the role of a minor actor, taking on a humble job, barely noticed by society, yet dedicated to conducting himself with integrity and dignity. Anonymity only bothers the part of ourselves caught up in feeling insignificant.

The self-centered *I* can be transcended in such a way that we continue to safeguard our interests and rights as individuals, while enjoying the emotional and physical advantages of being united for a common purpose as part of the community and nation. When egos clash in government, corporations, and institutions, it is to our detriment that the main consideration is usually for who comes out on top, not that truth or justice be served. While we need to have a personal *I* to interact with each other, we appear to be losing perspective, in this highly complex and individualistic society, of the place of this *I* in the great design of nature and existence.

In narcissism, nothing is held sacred, certainly not nature, not even God who is held under the thrall of what is expected of Him, rescue, validation, and redemption—of *me*.

In self-protection and insecurity, we keep the *I* at the center. We make a claim to power to save face and to avoid recognition of the saboteur within. The more we put the *I* out in front, the more we are blind to the elements of self-sabotage.

All this *I* business is our false pride, our buttered-up self-image, comprising our illusion of who we think we are, how we think things are, and how we want them to be, with our own pre-eminence as first priority. Were the doorman of a fancy hotel to embody this attitude, his self-image would be immensely gratified when little children, impressed by his gold-braided costume and decorous manner, mistook him as the host and proprietor.

An obvious byproduct of shallow self-centeredness, along with faulty judgment and irrational behavior, is pride. Pride is insidious. It can worm its way into the highest offices in the land as easily as the cardboard home of a derelict whose stubbornness may have led him into his predicament. Those in greatest denial of their investment in self-image are often those with the most pride in their humility. "In reality," Benjamin Franklin wrote in *The Autobiography,* "there is, perhaps, no one of our natural passions so hard to subdue as pride." As for humility, he added, "I cannot boast of much success in acquiring the *reality* of this virtue, but I had a good deal with regard to the *appearance* of it."[3.] Thus did Franklin take the measure of his pride; considering his greatness, he might have held it to a draw. It is not surprising, given the infantile egocentricity we bring into the world, that long after Franklin's refreshing candor so many of us exhibit a few cracks of humility only when forced by circumstances to swallow our pride.

The relationship between appropriate behavior and childish self-interest is well established in psychological theory. Child researcher Jean Piaget reaffirmed this in *The Moral Judgment of the Child* when he wrote, "It is only by knowing our individual nature with its limitations as well as its resources that we grow capable of coming out of ourselves and collaborating with other individual natures."[4.]

Psychoanalyst Erik Erikson expressed concern about the growing irrationality of people—politicians and business leaders in particular—who scorn measured progress in favor of pursuing diverse agendas in a headlong rush that ignores tradition and patient resolve. The impatience and disdain for established procedures are vital clues that such individuals are propelled by the desire to enrich or to exalt themselves. We wouldn't be so influenced by such self-serving people if we didn't have our own secret readiness, through our identification with them, to exalt ourselves.

In *Insight and Responsibility*, Erikson wrote that a shift in self-awareness "implies a fundamental new ethical orientation of adult man's relationship to childhood: to his own childhood, now behind and within him; to his own child before him; and to every man's children around him."[5] Erikson alluded to the futility of studying world history without reference to the influence of childhood, and he believed that the refusal of historians "to consider the historical relevance of human childhood can be due only to that deeper and more universal emotional aversion and repression which Freud himself foresaw."[6] The key to progress, he wrote, is to help each generation face the conflict "between its ethical and rational aims and its infantile fixations."[7]

Erikson believed in "new models of fraternal behavior" that would make it possible for individuals "to contribute true knowledge and genuine experience without assuming an authoritative stance beyond their actual competence and genuine inner authority."[8] His work was dedicated to the proposition that, despite poor or difficult childhoods, individuals can rise into fulfillment, creativity, and greatness through the process of deepening self-knowledge. Men and women in power, he wrote, must give "absolute priority" to the one effort that can keep a democratic country healthy—the effort to summon forth the potential intelligence of the younger generation. Perhaps the greatest knowledge, and the best challenge to our intelligence, consists of what our inner defenses are so determined to hide from us—the extent of our narcissism and the mechanisms of our self-defeat.

The problem of self-absorption was noted by author Will Henry in an essay, "A Time to Talk of Heroes," written in 1984 in response to what he saw as a dismal trend in the western novel, in which the central characters were no longer genuine heroes, nor honorable men and women, nor even antiheroes, but sociopathic scum. "Without heroes, there can be no hope," Henry believed.[9.] Every one of his fifty-three books was written with a hero, because it was his credo that no one wins when real heroes lose.

Psychiatrist Alexander Lowen noted that narcissism had become much more prevalent in the culture of the late 20th century than it was in the 1940s when he began his practice. He wrote in *Narcissism: Denial of the True Self:* "When wealth occupies a higher position than wisdom, when notoriety is admired more than dignity, when success is more important than self-respect, the culture overvalues 'image' and must be regarded as narcissistic."[10.]

Modern art, too, has become an homage to extreme individualism, in which the individual's personal, subjective interpretation is regarded with inordinate respect, and little or no distinction is made for whether that interpretation or representation is sacred, neurotic, or even psychopathic. It is a bit like being enthralled by a baby's crayon scrawls and honoring the baby for being so special. Being honored as special is exactly what a baby expects and a narcissist lives for

Folly Need Not Be Repeated

Modern influences certainly have a destabilizing influence on our psyche. In the past, humanity's egotistic nature was more easily held in check in tribes, small towns, and communities. Our ancestors felt more bonded to a group, more accountable to each other, and more susceptible to shame. They couldn't hide themselves from others as we can in this anonymous society.

We no longer have the extended family or the tribe to help us feel part of something greater than ourselves, to help us open our hearts and awaken compassion. Nature in its old splendor helped some to ponder the mystery of creation and transcend self-centeredness. Now urban dwellers can barely see the stars, obscured as they are at night by city lights.

Under today's influences, it is as if we live in an age of emotional deregulation. These modern influences include rapid changes in technology, urbanization and the breakup of the nuclear family, mass advertising's appeal to our base oral instincts, media that cater to passivity, sensationalism, and voyeurism, and the loss of contact with nature and tradition.

Consumerism gathers much of its appeal from our desperation to impress others (and ourselves) with the extent of what we *have,* because we are so uncertain of the value of who we *are.* Through acquisitions and materialism, we search for ways to validate ourselves, increase our self-importance, and also to distract ourselves, in order to ward off inner feelings of having no significance or value whatsoever. A *me-first* entitlement attitude spreads like metastasizing cancer.

Never before have so many people experienced such extensive freedoms, wealth, and leisure, and had to cope with the invasive impact of technology, consumerism, and marketing. Meanwhile, the former behavioral restraints of authority and religion are losing their power of intimidation and control. As movies, television, and media throw back the boundaries of propriety, our inner restraints of conscience and moral imperative lose their regulatory power over our drive for pleasure and sensationalism. Yet inner boundaries are necessary for personal integrity and self-regulation.

The history of nations and empires reveals that great powers crumble and decline from within. These powers may be affected, of course, by outside factors such as shifting alliances and populations, changing ideologies and technologies, and competition. Invariably, however, their declines had much to do with psychological elements such as pride, paranoia, and greed. It appears that leaders and citizens of these states and empires succumbed to dark forces of the psyche that were beyond the reach of their current knowledge. Historian Barbara Tuchman showed in *The March of Folly: From Troy to Vietnam* how various governments throughout history pursued self-defeating policies because objective and wise assessments were sabotaged by the illusions, stubbornness, and pride of government leaders.[11.]

Such self-sabotage need not be continue to be humanity's Achilles' Heel. Though the impact of modern challenges renders us more alone, separated, and frightened, we have to see how these challenges can be liberating if through them we are prodded to raise our consciousness.

We now have the knowledge that sees into the roots of our negative emotions and self-defeating reactions. We also have the information superhighway to drop this knowledge in the lap of every citizen. What we don't have, however, is the will to enlighten ourselves because, through our investment in self-image, we prefer to enshrine rather than dethrone our illusions of ourselves.

"Love thy neighbor as thyself" is an exhortation to value and respect others as we value and respect ourselves. If we are unable to respect and love ourselves, then something is blocking us; it is not the neighbor's fault. We are blocked because we are tangled up in painful convictions that we are less than others, that others see us as inferior, that others get more than us, or that the world is indifferent to us. We are entangled in self-denial and self-hatred. These negative emotions will begin to unravel with the coming emergence from our childhood hangover and recognition of our true self.

CHAPTER 4

The Nature of Passivity

Through social security, national security, and financial security, we have created a society that tries not only to protect us but to profit as well from fear and fate. When someone slips on a banana peel, he looks around for a person to sue and hobbles to the nearest lawyer to capitalize on his misfortune. We have monetized fate, so that comfort is taken and profits are made in protections such as life and health insurance, hi-tech hospitals, home security systems, private security forces, handguns and assault rifles, lawyers and lawsuits, and the military-industrial complex.

So why are we so enamored of security? We all have leftover fears from childhood of being abandoned, starved, unloved, and helpless. A human child spends a longer time in relative stages of helplessness than any other creature. In his early years he has limited mobility and cannot communicate effectively. Most animals leave the nest or lair after several months or a year or two, but a human being requires about fifteen years of parental support before he is mature and independent enough to thrive on his own. This long maturation is required for the development of the sophisticated human brain and nervous system. Thus traits and fears associated with dependency have a long time in which to become imprinted in the psyche, contributing to the extent in which we are fixated emotionally on past stages of our development.

As children, we endured passive experiences of having to submit to the will of someone else, of being denied and deprived, controlled and dominated. We were told what we could and could not do, and our attempts to act independently were often met with disapproval and punishment. We were rewarded for controlling our emotions and impulses, and we won approval for obeying without protest.

As adults we continue to feel controlled by others, by our jobs, and by the requirements of daily life. We feel helpless in certain contexts—helpless to influence institutions or government, to improve our circumstances in life, to overcome disease or ill health, to break habits and refrain from certain behaviors, and to control our anger and our consumption of food, drugs, and alcohol.

Our struggle for autonomy can be compounded when, as children, we are expected to adopt without question the prevailing views of parents and society rather than being taught how to become our own authorities. Later, as adults, we may find ourselves swinging back and forth between undue compliance with authority or in rebellion against it. Or we may find ourselves trying in frustration to control others and make life conform to our will, defending against our own feelings of being controlled.

Either way, we come under the spell of authority figures or controlling influences and remain mired in feelings of helplessness and passivity. (As I use it, the word *passivity* encompasses self-sabotage, in the sense that it incorporates the painful predicament of being under the influence of our emotional attachments, particularly to feeling controlled or dominated, and the self-defeating consequences of reacting to them.)

An aspect of our passivity is the *cause-and-effect* point of view that children develop to explain how the world works and which lingers on in adults. A child experiences himself at the mercy of external events and agents that he believes make him feel the way he does. In other words, something happens and there is a direct effect: "Mom yells at me and I feel hurt; my brother kicks the cat and I get blamed; I go potty on the floor and Mommy gets mad; I say something bad and get punished." The child attempts to offset the passive, powerless sense that he must accept what happens to him by believing *he causes things to happen.* This is his "solution" for the conflict produced by the terrible feeling of complete helplessness. The child believes, for instance, "I caused Mom to reject and punish me because I was being bad; Mom is depressed because I didn't clean my room; Mom and Dad are fighting because I was bad."

While such cause-and-effect thinking is a compensation for feeling helpless, it ultimately works against us because it creates yet another way that we find ourselves at the mercy of situations and others. Cause and effect is part of our natural resistance to taking on responsibility and claiming our power. An individual may say, "If only you would change, I wouldn't feel this way," or "High unemployment is responsible for my career problems," or "I could have succeeded if she hadn't blocked my promotion," or "It's impossible to lose weight with all those food commercials on TV."

We frequently say, "He caused me to feel this way." In fact, no one *causes* you to feel a certain way. You are the one who takes on those feelings based on your own issues. It is true that others can *trigger* those feelings in you, but the feelings are already there inside you, ready at the slightest provocation to jump up and be experienced. When Joe Blow says something that you feel is offensive or provocative, observe your reaction. Say to yourself, "Look how I'm feeling angry (sad, offended, disgusted) after hearing what Joe said. Where does that come from in myself?"

While physical actions usually cause a predictable physical effect (throw a stone in the air, for instance, and it always comes down), interpersonal actions do *not* have to cause a predictable effect. If someone yells at you, you don't necessarily have to feel fearful or angry. Your reaction depends on your emotional strength, your willingness to understand yourself, and how you assimilate the experience.

New Understanding of Our Experiences

Escape from the passivity of cause-and-effect thinking involves seeing how we *co-create* and *interact with* the life we experience. The new physics of quantum mechanics, the study of subatomic matter, helps us to understand this interaction. At subatomic levels, we can't say that objective reality exists separate from ourselves. At these levels, mass and energy change unceasingly into each other. What we see is a factor of how we react to what we think is there. Thus our view of the universe is subjective. Physicists ask themselves, "Did a particle exist in such a position before we began an experiment to determine its position? Did we somehow create the particles that we are experimenting with?"

We need to ask similar kinds of questions when we apply the concepts of co-creation and mutual interaction to our relationships with the world and other people. For instance: "How have I contributed to the circumstances in which I am feeling neglected (or deprived, controlled, betrayed)? What is my role in this situation in which I want to believe I'm an innocent victim? Am I involved with this person (or this situation) in order to recreate some issue that is unresolved in myself?"

As we plunge deeper into these questions, the concepts of *co-creation* and *mutual interaction* defy common sense because they require us to see that we create, maintain, and reinforce sensations and experiences that are harmful and self-defeating. "Why would I be doing something that is harmful to myself?" we keep asking. "It doesn't make sense."

The new physics doesn't make sense either. "Commonsense contradictions, in fact, are at the heart of the new physics," writes Gary Zukav in his award-winning book on the subject. "They tell us again and again that the world may not be what we think it is. It may be much, much more."[1.]

So too is the configuration of our human nature much, much more than we have appreciated. So let's go deeper into this mystery.

The insights of new physics correspond with the insights brought into the psychological realm by the psychoanalyst Edmund Berlger, M.D. Bergler gave us a comprehensive framework for understanding our emotions as well as for seeing our unconscious collusion in the problems in our lives. He challenged the notion that we are simply passive recipients of what we experienced as children. He showed that we generate distorted impressions and deductions from inside ourselves about what is happening around us. We interact with and create our own personal reactions to the stimuli we see, forming conclusions that may diverge greatly from the reality of what is happening. These conclusions grow into fixed negative messages and expectations about ourselves and others. As children and as adults, we process the "facts" we perceive according to highly subjective interpretations.

The concept of co-creation and mutual interaction enables us to become responsible for our experiences, shows how we can overcome our passivity (the experience of being under the influence of our negative impressions and expectations), and helps eliminate self-sabotage. Here is an example.

George, a dentist, was a client who had a tendency to drink heavily at social events or parties. He said he needed alcohol in order to "come alive" and really enjoy himself. However, before these evenings had run their course, he frequently became obnoxious or got sick from drinking too much. The next day George would often have forgotten much of what took place at the party, and his wife would complain that his conduct had embarrassed her. "I don't want people to see me as a drunk," he said earnestly. "I want to be able to drink and not go over the edge with it."

I asked him, "How would you feel if you went to a party having decided not to drink?"

"Well, it hasn't happened for years. But I can tell you—I get bored. I look at them and see the same old faces and hear the same old small talk. I've heard it all before. I'm not good at it. Just let me go home, I say to myself, and watch TV."

I told him, "I want to show you how you contribute to creating that impression that the people are boring. As a child, you picked up your father's insecurity and lack of self-respect. As you've told me, your father felt like a nobody—completely insignificant and worthless. He would drink and became a show-off and a showboat around others to compensate for that feeling. Well, George, you have some of that in you. When you go to a social event, you are steeped in the feeling that you'll be seen as boring and insignificant unless you make a big splash and become the center of attention. But by drinking and becoming obnoxious, you become like your father and create the feeling of being a fool, which is the way you expect to be seen—the same way you saw your father.

"When you don't drink, you believe the problem is that the people you are with are boring and insignificant. You are seeing them as you really expect to be seen—as boring and insignificant—and as how you see yourself. The solution is, first, to acknowledge your attachment to the feeling of being seen in this negative manner; second, to get in touch with your feelings of having seen your father exhibit in this negative way and the emotional effect it had on you; third, to see that you are subjecting others to the same foolishness that you were subjected to, in order to identify with their shame and embarrassment; and, fourth, to understand that regarding yourself as an insignificant fool blocks you from seeing your true self and appreciating and loving who you are."

As another example of co-creation and mutual interaction, Tom and Grace are trying to help their daughter, Sally, with her homework. Sally interprets their intervention as an indication that she isn't smart enough to do it on her own. She feels bad about herself and resists cooperating with them. Tom and Grace genuinely have Sally's best interests at heart and hope she will benefit from their helpfulness. Unconsciously, however, she resists experiencing the situation from that perspective. She perceives "help" as an indication that she is inadequate, that her parents must intervene because she is lacking in intelligence.

Sally is not aware of her secret willingness to be judged negatively. She makes a subliminal claim-to-power defense: "I cause them to have to come to my rescue because I'm not smart enough." She accepts the "fact" that she is not smart enough for the purpose of covering up her passive affinity for seeing herself as defective or unworthy.

In accepting her parents' help, Sally feels that something unpleasant is being done to her by them. She feels *acted upon* and slips into a deeper passivity. She may then begin to react passive-aggressively in other situations—replying caustically, being late, procrastinating on chores—under circumstances that baffle her parents. By resisting their help, she also fails to assimilate the lessons of her homework, and thus sabotages herself in this way. This pattern of passive-aggressively resisting help—based on her subjective interpretation of inadequacy—will be played out in her adult life, particularly in how she is apt to resist the support and love of others.

Sally is receiving and interpreting her parents help as an indication of her inadequacy, while her parents are offering their help without being aware of their daughter's reaction. Two intersecting points of view are happening simultaneously in an interactive dance. This is interaction, not cause and effect. Were Sally to see this, she would have the option to come into harmony with the experience of being helped and make it work to her benefit.

Interaction and co-creation mean we are always making choices in how to respond to situations. If something or someone affects us, we are allowing it to affect us, whether positively or negatively, consciously or unconsciously. We react emotionally to stimuli from our own unique perspective. We feel controlled (or deprived, rejected, criticized, and so on) in a given situation due to our willingness to feel controlled. Thus, we are co-creators in our emotional and behavioral experiences rather than passive recipients of what life or people dish out.

The cause-and-effect mentality is revealed in statements such as, "He hurt me by staying away" and "You offended me with that remark." When we understand co-creation we might say instead, "I'm willing to feel hurt and offended by his actions," or "I can see by my negative reaction that I'm allowing myself to be affected by his remark." The intensity of our negative reaction to a given situation is within our power to regulate, especially when we see and understand how our negative reaction covers up our secret willingness to be hurt, offended, or otherwise victimized. Cause-and-effect thinking leads us to the conclusion that our feelings and actions are justified by difficult external conditions or that we are to blame because of physical, mental, or character flaws.

Quick to Feel Provoked

A cartoon shows a man sitting down for a job interview. The personnel director says with a neutral expression, "Your resume says that you've filed lawsuits against all your former employers. Is that true?" The man answers, "Are you trying to upset me?" This touchy fellow is a joke because he manages to feel provoked at every opportunity.

All of us feel provoked by challenging circumstances. I'm reminded of an incident a few years ago in front of the main Post Office in Santa Fe, New Mexico. A man muttering angrily to himself trudged diagonally across the street in front of me, requiring me to brake my vehicle and wait for him to pass. His rumpled agitation and general appearance indicated that he might be making his way from the nearby police station. Instead of looking away as he crossed in front of me, or at least maintaining a neutral expression, I caught his eye and shook my head in disgust. He swore at me and kicked the passenger door of my truck as he went by, leaving a small dent that I notice occasionally and humbly reflect upon.

Why did I get triggered by this man and shake my head in scorn? This was how, as I perceived it, my father and mother often saw me. All through childhood I was tormented with doubt about my value as a person. I often got "hit up" with impressions of being looked at with disgust and was burdened with the shame of being seen as defective and bad. My father was inclined to see me as a good-for-nothing scamp, just as his father had seen him in this negative way. My mother saw me as someone always messing up, starting with toilet training and continuing through my teenage indifference to household order and cleanliness. Consequently, I tended to judge others in a similar way, just as I saw myself in this way.

Through the awareness of interaction and co-creation, we understand our role and collusion in the experiences that produce our scorn, anger, or other reactions. A client told me once how resentful she felt toward her husband. "I'm furious at him," she said. "In lots of little ways he likes to be in charge. We bicker about how to decorate the house, even how to park the car, do the dishes, and take out the garbage. When he gives his opinion, I feel I have to resist. So much of my attention revolves around how he thinks and feels about what I do."

"Let's look at your part in this," I replied. "Begin to monitor and to observe *how you experience this situation through the feeling of being acted upon by him.* Although he too has issues and can be provoking, it is unlikely he intends to control you. You're the one who experiences him as a restricting, controlling influence. You do that because, emotionally, you're ready to take on that feeling at any opportunity, although you vigorously cover it up through your anger toward him and through your resistance to cooperating with him or seeing his point of view. Ultimately, your anger is a defense against your attachment to feeling controlled, meaning your anger is produced to cover up your willingness to 'take a hit' on feeling controlled."

Another client, Tom, also began to understand how his self-sabotage was co-created. His frequent angry outbursts revolved around feelings of being controlled and dominated by others, especially at work, and feelings of being held back and constricted. He went to his department-store job five minutes late one morning and saw the manager looking at him from a distance. Tom hurried off in the other direction, fearful he would get angry and defensive if the manager approached him. Later in the day Tom fumed with stifled rage when the manager told him that the day off Tom requested had been denied.

I said to Tom, "Your anger is a direct reaction to the feelings you take on of being passive to someone like your boss. You are attached to an emotional impression of being controlled by him and at his mercy, and your feelings of anger are designed to cover up and protest against this feeling.

"Meanwhile, your passivity, meaning your unconscious willingness to feel acted upon in a way that is constraining, is an aspect of your self-sabotage. And your defensive or aggressive reactions to this feeling could certainly get you in trouble with your boss. As well, you will feel this passivity in other areas, with your wife and friends. As you've said, you feel it when you're stuck waiting in traffic or in a line at the supermarket. All the while, you're likely to believe that your impatience and other negative reactions are justified by the trying circumstances in which you find yourself."

"I don't know any other way to feel," he snapped. "What am I supposed to do? Kiss their butts?"

"Just be aware that a part of you jumps in and takes on feelings of being held back and controlled. Try to observe that part. Stand back from it and see it like a software program in a computer. It's an unsatisfactory program but you keep running it. You are attached to the feeling of being controlled, so you have a secret willingness to play this program and thereby to keep experiencing the feeling of being controlled. Feeling controlled by others also reflects a pattern of self-oppression. You want to see and feel how you limit and squelch yourself. Seeing more clearly into your own self-inhibitions, you become less reactive to the impression of being controlled by others."

In understanding co-creation, we discover how our unconscious mind works against our best interests. We begin to explore pertinent questions such as: "Why did I do that? What was the underlying feeling? Where did that feeling come from? What's my real motive for wanting this? What am I secretly holding on to? How am I feeling about myself? How am I mistreating and limiting myself?"

Passivity's All-Consuming Embrace

Passive-aggressive behaviors are also indicators of our passivity. These are behaviors in which we passively withhold our cooperation or seek in other ways, often unconsciously, to frustrate the one we feel passive to. These include forgetting to do what was promised, being persistently late, delaying with excuses, acting stupidly or incompetently, retaliating in subtle ways, holding grudges, making sarcastic comments, declining to say yes or no, displaying ambivalence, making poor decisions, and refraining from expressing our needs and expectations. We might obligingly tell someone, "Oh yes, I'll take care of it, I'll do it," but, in being unaware that we really don't want to do it because of inner feelings of control and obligation, we conveniently forget our pledge.

More signs of being passive include:

1) feeling oppressed or persecuted by someone or something;

2) feeling we have to comply with the requests of others or agree with their opinions;

3) believing our independent thoughts, feelings, or behaviors will be disapproved of by others;

4) allowing ourselves to be emotionally or financially dependent on others;

5) feeling helpless and defeated;

6) saying *yes* when we want to say *no*; enduring situations without taking action;

7) borrowing someone else's belief system rather than making our own assessment of reality; assuming external authority knows more than we do (this surrendering to authority makes it easier to overlook or rationalize unethical or corrupt behaviors, as well as to be less responsible for our own behaviors and attitudes);

8) being swayed by political polls and tempted to follow the crowd; or believing the worst of others without proof, and thus being influenced by gossip and negative political advertising campaigns; believing naively that others have our best interests at heart and have no self-interest;

9) envying others; feeling passive to their material accumulations or accomplishments;

10) expecting the police, the government, or other authorities to solve all our problems;

11) relying on others to inspire us or push us into action;

12) giving undue authority to certain groups or adopting extreme ideological positions;

13) taking as fact the false promises of loved ones ("I'll take care of you forever," or "I'll never do that again," or "I'll stop drinking for good starting next week"), or believing the empty promises we make to ourselves (to exercise more, to eat and drink less, to get our act together);

14) feeling confused about what we want in life and in what direction we should go.

Much of our self-sabotage is a result of this passivity, which incorporates our (unconscious) giving of consent to being intimidated, controlled, unduly influenced, held back, restrained, made to wait, thwarted, and having to endure. Helplessness is an aspect of passivity. To make a decision based on avoidance is a form of passivity, just as making a rash decision out of inappropriate anger is a consequence of passivity. Blaming is a form of passivity, as is the entitlement attitude which is the refusal to take responsibility for one's capability or purpose in the world.

Both men and women have issues with passivity, although styles of passivity can differ along gender lines. As a generalization, men are more likely to indulge in feelings of what they may lose (status, skills, virility), while women are more tempted to resort to feelings of missing out on something (participation, romance, love). In a wider sense, passivity is a consequence of our emotional attachments to feeling loss, deprival, refusal, rejection, and criticism. It is also an expression of our difficulty in orienting ourselves in the world without something to react against or something to oppose.

Ultimately, passivity is a negation of our own self—of our authority, power, perspectives, ideas, and visions. It is a major block to knowing our true self.

Unaware of our self-negation and the underlying passivity that results from it, we point to aggression as the cause of our problem. For example, it is popular to believe that domestic violence is caused by aggression and rage. But what prompts the aggression and rage? Self-hatred, passivity, and a sense of victimization underlie the consciousness of both the recipient of the violence *and* the perpetrator. A typical perpetrator in domestic-violence cases is a male who believes ironically that *he is the one being victimized and abused* by his spouse or girlfriend, his children, and life in general. He believes his partner, his children, and others don't understand him, don't respect him enough, and make too many demands on him (mirroring how he feels about himself). He holds them accountable for his frustration, anger, sense of helplessness, and powerlessness. In acting out his violent reactions, he unconsciously identifies with his partner's feelings of being violated, reduced, and negated, feelings that he himself is secretly attached to. In other words, his violence is a reaction to, and a symptom of, his own entanglement in passive feelings such as worthlessness and helplessness. Considering that most abusers were themselves abused as children, he imposes on his partner the mistreatment he received as a child, recreating through her the helplessness of being at the mercy of the cruel, demeaning other and the pain of being treated with an utter contempt. Inwardly, he abuses himself through self-rejection and self-hatred.

There are other ways we cover up passivity with aggressive or angry behavior. For example, a wife who is feeling controlled by her husband retaliates by demeaning his character, a teenager mired in a feeling of worthlessness strikes out with his graffiti to denigrate what others value, and an adolescent who is feeling refused by his parents feels entitled to steal money from them to get what he wants. In all these cases, it appears at first glance that the aggressive behaviors are the primary problem. However, as I said, the aggression is *a pseudo-aggressive reaction* to underlying passivity.

Doing nothing when such inertia is inappropriate is also passivity, a distinctive form of self-sabotage. Some people want to imagine that in their passivity they are entirely innocent of any culpability or responsibility. In doing nothing, however, we are making a choice, even if it is unconscious. For instance, in letting others make important decisions for us, we abdicate responsibility and make a choice to allow ourselves to be passively controlled and taken in. In this self-sabotage, we allow ourselves to be led down the garden path to find disappointment or even disaster.

As another example of this kind of passivity, a TV repairman I had as a client, a happily married man, showed up once at a house where a scantily-clad woman flirted with him as he worked on her TV. Before he could organize his thoughts and feelings, he had come under her spell, feeling enthralled and aroused by her presence. She stayed at his side for thirty minutes, talking to him and handing him tools, while his heart raced and his passions soared. He felt completely at the mercy of however far she was willing to take this encounter, and he came exceedingly close to having sex with her. If the woman had invited him into her bedroom, he told me, he would have been unable to resist. Yet, had this happened, he would be making a decision, however much it was shrouded in his passivity, to be unfaithful to his wife.

The issue here was not so much with sex and betrayal as with power and helplessness. This man grew up with a weak father and a strong, dominating mother who, even when he was in his mid-teens, insisted on choosing the style of clothes he wore. He had felt very passive toward his mother and, as an adult, took on this feeling in the presence of strong women. He came under the influence of the seductress not because she was necessarily so strong or beautiful but because he was prepared emotionally to allow her to dominate the encounter. So a choice was made, although unconscious, to react passively to her. Had she attempted to have sex with him, his acquiescence would have represented a choice on his part, though he might not know when the choice was made and might later try to assuage any guilt by believing he was innocently seduced.

Our lives are filled with such passivity. A friend calls to ask you out; though you prefer to stay home, you find yourself going along with the request. Your boss asks you to do an assignment; you would have preferred an alternate task, yet you say nothing and do as requested. Even major life events can be experienced passively, such as being swayed to marry a person you feel ambivalent about but who others think is perfect for you.

Ask yourself how conscious you have been of making a choice in important situations. Do you find yourself in situations where things are just happening to you, where you have made a choice not to make a choice? It is in understanding passivity at this depth, and seeing what it means to be self-responsible in this way, to understand the allure of passivity, that you become more conscious of how to avoid this form of self-sabotage.

Because of our passivity, we like to generate the impression of having power or being powerful. Early humans believed their sacrifices appeased the gods. They felt the need to *do something* to protect themselves, rather than to sit around feeling helpless to whimsical gods and capricious expressions of nature. Nowadays, a person might say, "I healed that person through my prayers," or "His life would have been a mess if I hadn't come along." People are always making claims to power. For instance, someone driving a car gets hit from behind and says to himself, "I knew it! It's my fault! I should have just stayed home today!" He makes this claim as a defense against the dreaded feeling of being helpless in the face of fate.

Our first claims to power are made at a very young age. To compensate for the painful experience in childhood of being utterly helpless, the child, instead of meekly acquiescing to his fate, manages to salvage an illusion of power through the feeling that, "Nobody is forcing me; I am making a decision to comply with this request (i.e. Mom's demands that I not throw my food on the floor) because *I* choose to do so." Now he feels comfortable eating his mashed peas, secure in his belief he has chosen to do so despite their horrid taste, while he conveniently overlooks the presence of mom standing nearby ready to shovel the peas down his throat should he pursue last week's pattern and spit them on the floor.

Another claim to power is exercised through what has been called the *unconscious repetition compulsion*. This is the compulsion to do to others what we have passively experienced (i.e. adults who were abused as children are at high risk to become abusers of their own children). We repeat *actively* what we have felt forced to endure *passively*, thereby mitigating the original offense to our narcissism. For instance, a boy required to sit in the dentist's chair, enduring the "agony" of having a tooth drilled, might come home and play dentist with his little sister, having her passively lie on the floor, open her mouth, and endure his "treatment."

The experience of dieting can illustrate how we collude in feelings of being controlled. Being on a diet not only provides an opportunity to feel deprived and refused but leaves many of us feeling controlled and forced to submit to the requirements of the diet. A diet thus represents submission to a program or submission to a parent or spouse who is requiring us to be on the program. Taking this emotional interpretation, we resist the program and rebel against the diet, just as we may have rebelled directly or indirectly against feeling controlled by our parents. We will also resist attending dieting or therapy programs out of feeling forced to submit to a person or organization.

The person who finds himself out of control with his life and behaviors sets himself up for others to take over and regulate his behaviors for him. Kathy, for example, was struggling to regulate her life. An anorexic, she starved herself and exhibited outbursts of emotional instability, convincing others that she couldn't function independently. Eventually, her behavior became so self-destructive that her family stepped in and put her in a psychiatric center. Whereas this woman once depended on her family for regulation, protesting all the while how much she hated that control, she now required a psychiatric center, a form of external control that was even more rigid.

The childish part of ourselves is looking to recreate parental authority and direction, even while a part of us rebels against it. Millions of people set themselves up to be regulated by outside sources, whether that be a parent, a spouse, a health professional, psychics, an ideology, a religion, a group, or some system or program that regulates their behavior or dictates how they should live.

Authoritarian styles of government or religion are based on the parent-child model. In such systems, we are expected to obey and learn from someone who is in charge of us, who claims to know what is best for us, and who instructs us in how to live our lives. We can even establish a version of the parent-child model with a democratic government, if we are dependent on the government for financial support or moral direction, or to make us feel safe. Under this model, the government becomes, in an emotional sense, protector and provider of the citizen, while the citizen, in exchange for security, turns over more of his own autonomy than is wise. A democratic system tainted by the parent-child model is more likely to engender and to tolerate corruption because of the unconscious passivity of the citizens.

Authoritarian systems will continue to exist as long as people are essentially passive and willing to be led and directed by others in exchange for the security and comfort of external regulation. Emotionally, it is threatening to us to become our own authority, to begin to think for ourselves, find our own answers, make our own mistakes, and trust in ourselves at this level. So we resist the co-creation model even though it is so liberating.

Society As Our Scapegoat

Often we feel that society is contributing to our conflicts and failures. Twenty years ago I was convinced that the foibles of parents, bosses, politicians, and insensitive capitalists, in that order, were to blame for my dissatisfactions in life. My suffering reflected my unconscious determination to feed on feelings of being ignored, neglected, and unappreciated. My existential misery persisted and drove me to find deeper answers. Real transformation began as I understood the concept of co-creation and interaction. I saw that society with its corruption and injustices simply reflected my (our) psychology and evolvement. I saw how determined I was to hold in place my own self-negation and self-rejection.

Through the lens of interaction, we see that society and culture can indeed act on us in unproductive ways. But we also contribute to the state of the society. Both are true. We can't say one causes the other. For instance, the media produce violent movies and television, just the kind of entertainment that fascinates us most. Nothing is imposed upon us without our willingness to accept it. We are the ones who live on the surface of ourselves and are thus eager consumers of all sorts of false promises and superficial values. Many of us oppose our society's open displays of sexuality, but nonetheless we accept it as a collective culture. I believe that we accept corruption in Washington, particularly the influence of special-interest money, because we tolerate (we don't strive to eradicate) the corruption (our collusion with the negative) within ourselves.

Some individuals want to believe that society's rules and regulations block self-expression. But we conform when culture tells us to wear certain styles, look a prescribed way, and believe in consumer values. The media persuade us to lose weight and be skinny, and as we oblige we contribute to the resulting food disorders. The bottom line is that we give our consent, through our own ignorance and passivity, to these models of how we are supposed to be.

Instead of conforming, some of us rebel. In the 1960's, young radicals rebelled against bourgeoisie values. In adopting polarized confrontation to challenge authority, they transferred their unresolved emotional experiences with their parents (feeling restricted and forced to accept parents' values) onto the culture, with the unconscious intent of repeating (but not resolving) experiences of control and disapproval. The young rebels were acting out an interaction with the culture based on opposition, the kind of interaction they had with their parents. Each of us is likely to perceive culture as we perceived our parents. If we rebelled against our parents, we are likely to rebel against culture, or at least to resist passive-aggressively the feeling of being consumed by it. But rebellion will not be successful when contaminated by such infantile aspects. If we were passive with our parents, then we are passive with the culture and we can't discern or challenge its falsities.

The most powerful rebellion, the one of lasting significance and value, is the one that you and I foment within ourselves, where we overthrow our self-sabotage—our self-negation, passivity, defenses, superficial self-image, and our attachments to negative feelings and impressions.

Some people say that authoritarian influences in society such as the rule of experts and hierarchic structures make it hard for us to trust and believe in ourselves. But these structures are in place because of our propensity to distrust ourselves (a distrust which exacerbates our passivity) and our feelings, ideas, and visions. Conversely, we use the existence of a so-called authoritarian structure as a rationalization for our distrust and passivity. "I'm not passive and self-negating," the individual proclaims, "I am simply standing here in the pecking order doing what's expected of me." When we endeavor to root out the distrust and the mother lodes of irrationality within ourselves, we come to know that it is not society but our particular brand of subjective interaction with it that instigates our malaise.

If we see the truth about ourselves and refuse to act, we suffer guilt for our passivity and lack of will. If we resolve to act, we have to mobilize our inner forces and generate all our courage and will to move us through resistance to new birth and growth. It seems easier to pretend we don't know what is going on. Or we can blame culture or society rather than face ourselves. But this avoidance of self-responsibility is risky and likely to entail much emotional suffering, especially in the form of discontent, loss of self-regulation, and self-sabotage.

The self-responsible person doesn't fight society. He observes it, participates in what is satisfying, and ignores or opposes what is out of balance. He sees that others use their convictions of being oppressed or unjustly treated as excuses to suffer. He does not idolize individuals or bow to ideologies. He listens to figures of authority and weighs their words against his own opinions. If he acts on his own authority and discovers he has miscalculated, he is able to accept and assimilate the consequences of his actions.

The cause-and-effect mentality is like a jail cell in which we have locked ourselves. Such limited awareness makes us captive to our own passivity, prompting us to conform or to rebel but always leaving us feeling that we are being *acted upon* by forces and elements outside ourselves. In contrast, the new perspective of interaction or co-creation frees us from the clutches of fate and reveals the pathway to our destiny. It provides us with essential and powerful insight about how we are accountable for the ways we falter and sabotage ourselves.

CHAPTER 5

Victims of Ourselves

The victim mentality described in this chapter is shared by all humanity and accounts for much human misery and self-sabotage. It is a kind of emotional bondage that blocks fulfillment of our potential and represents an abdication of sovereignty over our thoughts, feelings, and behaviors.

Much has been said and written about this mentality and its negative impact on individuals and society. In this chapter, we look deeper into the tendency to take on victim feelings and see more clearly the connection between the victim mentality and self-sabotage.

How do we account for the great contradictions that bedevil our lives? We strive to be positive but are enmeshed in the negative. We want to be masters of our selves but are puppets of our conditioning, compulsions, and secret agendas. We dream of emotional freedom as we surrender to inner tyranny. The victim mentality is a byproduct of these contradictions. It is also a consequence of our inability to see more objectively into the nature of reality and into the nature of our being.

This mentality has its origins in childhood when, as babies and adolescents, we misinterpreted our experiences in such a way as to feel refused, controlled, and rejected even when that wasn't our parents' intent. As adults, we unconsciously retain emotional memories of that experience. However, because the

experience remains unconscious, we are hindered from knowing ourselves in greater depth. Often, we don't know what we
are experiencing other than some vague sense of contentment
or unhappiness. We may be riddled with self-doubt, self-criticism, and self-rejection and not be able to guide ourselves out
of this morass because our experience of ourselves is too vague
and confused. That is because we experience ourselves by way
of superficial impressions, borrowed beliefs, and a wide range of
defenses.

Experience, not behavior, is fundamental to our very being,
richer in our essence, and a pathway to our soul. Yet a parent
may not know what his children are experiencing. He may
think he knows, but he is likely to be knowing them largely
through his own projections and identifications. A kind, con-
siderate husband may not know how his wife of forty years is
experiencing herself. Deep pain is felt by marriage partners
when each is unable to communicate his and her experience to
themselves and to each other. And so on.

The point is this: when you are not fully alert to what you
are experiencing, you won't see or feel the extent to which negative impressions are infiltrating your life, generating a victim
mentality.

Since we have forgotten the experience of childhood, let us
try to imagine how it was. Some aspects of our infantile state of
mind have already been described in preceding chapters, and a
further elaboration follows.

The baby begins life with a built-in conflict: he is infused
with a sense of being one with outer reality, being unable to distinguish himself as a separate entity. In his mind, everything
good is self-produced and self-bestowed, and thus there is no
need for gratitude toward the caretaker or even acknowledgment. Because of his mother's "intrusiveness" and his dependence on her, the feeling of "oneness" is eroded and she is felt in
some sense to be against him. In part his mother is experienced

by him as something bad, a giantess of the nursery who intrudes upon him in opposition to his feelings and wishes.

More hurt is felt by the child when his desire for the breast or the bottle is not instantly fulfilled (as described earlier). A wait of a few minutes can seem like eternity because the child has no ability to understand the relativity of time. Hence, mother not only opposes him but is also refusing.

The baby is frustrated by his passive dependence on getting milk. He is passively subjected to a time schedule for meals and, most humiliating of all, must undergo the passively experienced "tragedy" of weaning. Meanwhile, the functions of urination, defecation, and sleep (experienced as normal by an adult) are felt quite differently by the child. Something irresistible drains parts of his body or forces him to expel part of himself. Something makes him go to sleep. He develops several fears: of starvation, created by his exaggeration of the hardship of waiting even a few seconds for breast or bottle; of being devoured, a projection of his own aggressive designs upon the nipple; of being choked by the mother's breast or body; and of being drained, a result of his "helplessness" in the elimination process. The child even feels victimized by the oral intrusion and "piercing" of the nipple, although his oral gratification somewhat alleviates the displeasure. His misunderstandings of these experiences is understandable, given how they defy his only measuring rod—his "oneness" with outer reality.

As months go by, the child is forced by reality to acknowledge the mother's generosity and kindness. But this recognition, instead of lessening the child's conflict, can serve to intensify it. Now he feels ambivalence toward his mother, with both friendly and unfriendly feelings toward her doing battle within him at the same time.

As counter-measures to feeling passive, he fights back on the oral and anal levels. On the oral level, he cries, screams, protests, vomits, and occasionally refuses food. On the anal level, his trick is retention. He stubbornly refuses to produce the feces desired by mother. Later, as an adult, he may suffer constipation when emotionally challenged.

In the first eighteen months of life, the baby's consciousness is in "oneness," meaning that all of existence consists only of himself. Next, in the anal stage, the baby is in "twoness," meaning he expands his consciousness to include his mother and she is recognized as a viable entity existing outside himself. Finally, in the genital stage, the child is in "threeness" and thus emotionally involved in a new order, the triangle of mother, father and child. A sense of himself as a separate entity is taking form.

These three stages correspond to the three categories of primary emotions discussed in Chapter 2, with the oral stage corresponding to the complete range of deprival issues, the anal stage to control issues, and the genital stage to rejection issues.

In this third stage, boys see father as a rival for mother's affection and may feel unloved and rejected as they see or imagine mother's affection going more to father or other family members. Girls feel acutely any deficiency of love and attention from their father, either directly from the father or indirectly through mother's experience of feeling unappreciated or unloved by her husband. Both boys and girls are prepared emotionally to embellish on feeling unloved, even when parents are kind and decent.

We carry these emotional attachments from childhood into our adult years and we are prepared to experience them anew in the different contexts of our lives. We become beggars, slaves, and orphans, exhibiting our own distinct brands of the victim mentality. In a thousand different ways, we are ready to feel like beggars (oral stage—deprived or refused), slaves (anal stage—controlled or dominated), and orphans (genital stage—rejected, discounted, pushed aside).

How does this relate to you? Feeling like a beggar, slave, and orphan can be so subtle that you may not have imagined yourself in such terms. Do you feel constrained or enslaved at work? Do you feel lonely and separate, orphaned by your spouse, parents, or community? Do you go around begging for more benefits in the form of income, recognition, and love to feel okay about yourself? Do you blame others or outside circumstances for not making more money, being more successful? Do you feel certain people are not supporting you or that they wish you ill? Do you feel the "system" is stacked against you?

We know we tend to be subjective and take things personally. We feel that much of what we experience opposes our wishes in some way. A sense of being victims can overtake us even in situations where we know we ought to be able to manage without emotional disruption. One man is furious at his wife because she becomes distracted and doesn't listen to him talking while he is driving. A woman complains repeatedly that her husband doesn't kiss her first thing in the morning. An office worker is furious that his friends, through a misunderstanding, fail to meet him one day for lunch. In each of these instances, the feeling of being a victim is produced by the unrecognized willingness to embellish upon feelings of being discounted or dismissed by others.

We become victims to ourselves if we don't discover who we are and what is available to us. Let us try to understand this by imaging a computer system, a wonderful desk-top workstation capable of an output that thirty years ago required the efforts of one hundred people or more. If we compare this workstation to ourselves, we see that the thoughts or images in our mind at any moment have their counterpart in the text or images on the computer's monitor. The text or image that appears on the video screen gives us the reading we need to work the system, just as our thoughts give us a reading and orientation for the world around us. The unconscious part of us is analogous to the functions, data, and programming stored on the computer's hard drive. We benefit by knowing about our unconscious aspects, just as we do by knowing all of the computer's tools and functions. How can we expect to make the best use of a computer without knowing about, or having access to, its functions, data, and tools? As I have been saying, eliminating self-sabotage depends on how well we understand ourselves, experience ourselves, and access vital information that has been unconscious.

We have made life very complicated, in step with the technological systems we have created. If we don't raise our intelligence of inner processes (tools and functions such as creativity, imagination, the will, the visual drive, intuition, and other extra-sensory faculties), we will be victimized by our lack of inner development. On the external level, we can see how we have been victimized by marketing and advertising (smoke cigarettes, eat fatty foods). The drive to make us voracious consumers can be thwarted by our growing intelligence into these processes of manipulation.

The elements of self-sabotage that reside within us are like bugs and quirks in a computer system. It helps us to see that our self-sabotage is like a technical problem and not an indication of a lack of goodness and value within us. If we don't see self-sabotage with some objectivity, we can become convinced emotionally, under its influence, that we are bad, unworthy, and useless. We allow these impressions to define who we are. It feels as if the bugs and quirks are us, like poisons that have permeated our system, rather than anomalies that can be identified, isolated, and eliminated from an otherwise healthy body and intelligence. Use of the computer metaphor helps us to be more objective, to see that the problem is not with ourselves, not with the essence of who we are, but with the random bugs or rogue quirks that plague the system.

Emotional anomalies, devastating though they can be in producing self-sabotage, are neither good nor bad—they just are. We feel them to be bad. But objectively or clinically, they are simply emotional configurations that can be eliminated, just as a virus can be eliminated with the right medical applications. They simply exist as an aspect of our human nature, through no fault of our own. Nonetheless, without insight, we become victims of them and thus victims of life.

Some psychologists teach confrontation and assertiveness—what they call "empowerment"—as a way to deal with the feelings of being a victim. But such an approach can provide official sanction for the tendency we have to react inappropriately to others. For instance, a typical person who is lacking in assertiveness *overreacts inwardly* to feeling refused, controlled, or rejected. He experiences frustration, anger, and the desire for revenge, though he keeps those feeling to himself or else complains to others who aren't directly involved in his conflict. If he angrily confronts those he believes are opposing him, he is only making visible the negativity that is stewing inside him. When an individual reacts this way, he may initially feel better for his aggression, though typically he will later feel guilty for it.

As an example, a young man driving on the freeway shoots and kills an older man who recklessly cut him off in traffic. The gunman pursues his victim for several miles before shooting him in the back of the head from fifty feet away. This is, of course, an extreme reaction, but it contains the same unconscious elements, minus the self-control, that would be involved in a less severe reaction. If the young driver had understood his emotional nature and the mechanism whereby he reacts in righteous indignation to feeling victimized, he would have had more ability to maintain self-control. He obviously took it personally when the other driver cut him off, which was an emotional "mistake" in the first place. The young man may have been under the influence of various emotional challenges. He may have been feeling cut off, cut down, reduced, or pushed around by a girlfriend, parents, boss, or a teacher. He may have been harboring feelings of being discounted, neglected, or rejected.

Suddenly, as the other driver cuts in front of him, all these emotions flood to the surface. The young man experiences anger, rage, and an enormous sense of being victimized. This powerful negative reaction, however, is a defense against an acknowledgment of his own passivity, meaning the extent to which he was prepared to soak up and "take a hit" on feeling discounted, cut off, and pushed aside. His overreaction is the self-sabotage, an act of "pseudo-aggression"—a phony attempt to "prove" how much he hates being treated in this manner. Now the older driver becomes the target of his pent-up emotional outburst. The young man displaces all his own emotional issues, in the form of this pseudo-aggressive reaction, onto the other driver.

The greater the unconscious attachment to feeling discounted and pushed aside, the more self-defeating the protest or defense is likely to become. The gunman certainly takes his protest to the limit when he pulls his handgun out of the glove compartment and takes off after his "tormenter." While his behavior cannot be condoned and must be punished, it nonetheless can be understood.

Confrontation that is a reaction to one's deep-rooted sense of victimization is not appropriate. We call this "dumping your stuff" on others. It doesn't win friends and influence people, and it doesn't resolve an individual's inner conflict. It is not confrontation one needs but insight into the existence and nature of one's victim mentality. When an individual becomes responsible for this condition and his reactions to it (seeing, for example, how he wants to use aggression to cover up his willingness to soak up feeling refused, controlled, or rejected), he can determine with greater clarity and more likelihood of success the best course of action to deal simultaneously with the internal and the external challenge.

A component of self-regulation is knowing the difference between healthy confrontation (or normal aggression), which is an appropriate response based on an objective assessment of fault or mistreatment, and a negative or exhibitionist reaction (pseudo-aggression) that springs out of an emotional attachment, is based on an inner readiness to feel offended or victimized, and is intended to cover up or defend against realization of the passivity or the attachment. As a general rule, healthy aggression is used only in self-defense, when the object of aggression is a real enemy rather than one of projection, misconception, or fantasy. The response of normal aggression corresponds with the degree of provocation, whereas phony or pseudo-aggression often far exceeds the provocation (e.g., shooting someone who has insulted you). Normal aggression is not easily provoked, while pseudo-aggression is.

A Lesson in Passing the Buck

The assimilation of inner knowledge of ourselves and our feelings strengthens our ability to see our victim mentality and step out from underneath it. Bill comes home from work after a bad day at the office. He had a disagreement with his boss and feels criticized, rejected, and generally victimized because, in his mind, his boss lacks sensitivity and appreciation for him. Brooding at home, Bill notices that his teenage son, Bobby, forgot to take out the garbage. Bill overreacts, berates his son for being irresponsible and lazy, and *displaces* onto his son the anger he feels toward his boss.

Bill's emotional outburst induces Bobby to buy into his father's accusations of being lazy and inconsiderate. Now Bobby feels worse about himself—like an orphan who is unappreciated, unloved, and rejected, similar to what his father felt earlier at work. To cover up his own unconscious readiness to indulge in feeling rejected, Bobby may make a claim-to-power defense, blame himself for being lazy and insensitive, and come into an inner conviction of being defective, flawed, and unworthy. Unconsciously, in self-sabotage, he may find ways to provoke more criticism and rejection from his father.

Of course, Bill's reaction against his son has little to do with his son's forgetfulness and everything to do with Bill's unpleasant encounter earlier that day with his boss. Bill spends the evening continuing to brood about his feelings toward his boss, imagining all the ways he might have retaliated or more effectively defended himself. While he is ensnared in feeling criticized and rejected, he is at the same time identifying with his son who is also experiencing the same feelings.

Bill has to understand that he is responsible for how he reacts to his boss and how he reacts to his son. While Bill may have genuine grievances with his boss, his displacement of his pseudo-aggression on to his son is a grievous injury to the innocent boy. It is a result of Bill's *transference* onto his boss of unresolved emotions stemming from how Bill experienced his own father.

As a youth, Bill felt criticized and rejected by his father. Bill has retained an orphan mentality and now transfers onto his boss the expectation of being treated as such. Bill's displacement onto his son is both a defense against, and a consequence of, his emotional willingness to indulge in feeling criticized and rejected. He does to his son what was done to him (by his father and boss) and then identifies with his son being "hit up" with those feelings. His aggressiveness with his son is also a reaction to the degree of passivity he experienced in the encounter with his boss.

Of course, this doesn't mean the solution is for Bill to react aggressively toward his boss. That could cost him his job. The solution is for Bill to understand his transference, see his own role in acting out the conflict with his boss, recognize how and why he passes the feeling of criticism and rejection on to his son, and work out his attachment to those feelings.

There is more self-sabotage here to be understood. Because of Bill's self-criticism and self-rejection, he may unconsciously provoke his boss to react negatively toward him. He will be negligent and careless in ways that upset his boss, thereby creating opportunities to replay the old criticism and rejection he felt with his father and to which he remains attached, while deepening feelings of being a victim of his boss and life in general.

Like Bill, we all *transfer* onto present circumstances emotions that are unresolved from the past. If Bill felt victimized in some way by his father, or some other authority figure from his past, he is under an *emotional compulsion*, as an adult, to continue to feel victimized by "father figures" and also, as a cover up for his passivity, to become pseudo-aggressive and victimize others, such as his son, who he feels to be under his authority.

To repeat, the solution for Bill requires that he come to know, not just intellectually but emotionally, that his anger with his son is a cover-up for his own attachment to feeling criticized and rejected. Since he experienced his father as criticizing and rejecting, Bill is ready to replay that passive relationship with his boss, and then to become like his father and be the aggressor in his relationship with his son. When Bill understands this, he begins to see through the illusion that he is justified in his negative feelings toward his boss and toward his son. He turns the spotlight on himself and sees how he displaces onto others the condemnation he directs toward himself. As a result, he can take responsibility for his reactions, learn to regulate them, and refrain from feeling victimized.

In psychological terms, Bill engaged in both *displacement* and *transference*. As described in Chapter 2, these defenses and reactions are unconscious phenomena through which we misinterpret current situations according to our emotional attachments and how we feel about ourselves. Understanding transference is especially vital for realizing how easily we can feel ourselves to be beggars, slaves, and orphans. To explain it again, transference is an unconscious process through which we repeatedly experience situations and relationships in a manner that revives emotional hurts from the past. When we don't see our transference, we are back into cause-and-effect thinking, believing our dissatisfaction, anger, selfishness, and urges for retaliation are justified by difficult external circumstances or the alleged ignorance and malice of others.

As mentioned, all of us have ways we felt victimized as children, even if these memories are repressed and we are not aware of them. Even if we had good parents, we felt emotionally challenged by the realization that we were helpless and subservient to the will of our parents. Our extreme self-centeredness with which we are born is at first offended by, and later begrudgingly resigned to, the requirement that we submit to our parents. Witness the tantrums of the "terrible twos" as a demonstration of how much we hated being toilet-trained, instructed, and socialized. Later, as adolescents and teenagers, it often feels so empowering and liberating to defy our parents, even when doing so is self-defeating.

Memories of our "subjugation" and helplessness don't magically disappear when we reach the age of consent or turn twenty-one. They persist, simmering beneath the surface, ready to be experienced repeatedly when opportunities arise. That is when we find ourselves face down in the hurt of being a beggar, slave, or orphan, at the mercy of those who seem to be indifferent to our existence.

Without the insight to resist it, the victim mentality is contagious and spreads through our ignorance. A college education, even a Ph.D. in psychology as it is now taught, is no immunization. A doctor or a ditch digger, of whatever race or color, could be the father in the example earlier of Bill and his son. Because of ignorance of unconscious dynamics, even the most upstanding citizens unwittingly contribute to family, community, and, by extension, national problems.

Starring in Our Victim Revue

Wallowing in feeling victimized has a certain appeal. Being a victim can be used to attract attention to oneself. Everyday people who may feel otherwise insignificant and unimportant relish the sympathy and recognition they receive in this role. In our self-centeredness we all like attention, and many prefer sympathy and even pity to what is felt as the only alternative— the sense of being anonymous. Doctors say that children and adults alike often make themselves sick in order to get attention and love.

People with a victim "mindset" can become paranoiac and unduly fearful of crime or, if their imagination is more unconventional, obsessed about the dangers of satanic cults and the threats of alien abductions. Alleged victims of such cults and abductions describe feeling controlled, passive, helpless, overwhelmed, violated, and terrorized. Individuals who are unconsciously attached to these feelings are determined to find explanations or "facts" in the environment that account for these feelings. When they find such an explanation, or when they concoct something that for them is believable, they have what they need to maintain and even to intensify their victim perspective. In these circumstances, the "facts" are subjective impressions that they use to buttress what they want secretly to feel.

Individuals who report being taken away against their will by aliens say they were overpowered, overwhelmed, and forced to submit to painful probing. This probing evokes feelings of helplessness, physical violation, and rape. I believe their conviction of having been abducted is induced by unconscious elaboration on what they experienced as infants and children— in the course of normal handling, lifting, and changing of diapers—at the mercy of what they experienced as powerful, controlling aliens, for in the throes of our infantile subjectivity we can experience our mother, father, and other caretakers as aliens, a feeling that is intensified by insensitive parents. Emotions and reactions dealing with the feeling of submitting passively to the parents' will—as well as to parents' touch, rules, regulations, criticism, reprimands, and spankings—can continue, in various degrees, to be mysteriously and profoundly experienced through the victim mentality.

It is helpful to look at these alleged abductions in symbolic terms, as representing a form of collective repressed memory of infantile passivity now transferred onto "aliens." As we imagine what aliens might be like, we unconsciously experience them from the vulnerable, passive position we had with our parents. Consciously, we may remember our parents as warm and nurturing, but unconsciously we have resistance to feeling that they helped us and supported our independent development. Why? As babies, we felt acted upon, controlled, and manipulated by normal parenting procedures and we remain emotionally attached to such passive feelings.

Some of us believe that our adult emotional problems stem from having been physically abused or sexually victimized as children. Controversy has arisen concerning the validity of repressed memories of alleged incest and ritual abuse. Some psychotherapists encourage their clients to consider the possibility that, repressed in the unconscious mind, reside factual memories of physical or sexual abuse. Such memories are then used to explain or excuse the emotional problems and self-sabotage of their clients. Therapists who look assiduously for past abuse may be identifying through their clients (in what is called *counter-transference*) with the feeling of being themselves innocent victims of some form of abuse. These experts don't take into account the tendency of children and adults to elaborate emotionally on feelings of being oppressed, dominated, and rejected, nor do they recognize our willingness to perpetuate this manner of experiencing reality.

Claire, a thirty-year-old office worker, believed she had been sexually abused as a child. As an adult, she had serious relationship problems, a long-standing eating disorder, and bouts of depression accompanied by suicidal fantasies. She exhibited sensitivity to criticism and isolated herself to avoid feeling controlled and overwhelmed. I used art therapy to help her access her feelings. She drew a series of pictures in which she was tied to a table and raped by a group of hooded men in long robes. She believed these pictures were evidence she had been subjected to some form of incestuous or ritualistic childhood abuse. But after studying the details of her emotional relationship with her parents, I concluded that these scenes or so-called memories were symbolic, like dream images.

These pictures represented Claire's unconscious attachment to feelings of being controlled, helpless, and at the mercy of powerful male figures. Claire believed that if she opened up her heart to men and revealed honest feelings, they would reject her, condemn her, and even destroy her. In one picture, she drew a hooded man extracting a heart from the breast of a female child. The picture depicted her emotional perception of her own predicament, that her parents would, as she put it, "cut out her heart" if she dared oppose them in any way. The picture might also represent how she lost her own self—her essence, her heart—in the process of accommodating the emotional needs of her parents.

Claire described her father as controlling and suffocating. He overwhelmed her with emotional neediness and, at the same time, demanded that she perform in the world according to his own perfectionist standards. Her mother was passive and nurturing, yet also critical and controlling in her attempts to help Claire deal with emotional upset.

As I have said, children often misinterpret their parents' behaviors, mistaking support or help as control or an indication the parents see them as inept. As well, many individuals come into the world with a weak emotional structure (just as some of us are less adept physically or intellectually) and fail to accommodate or neutralize the emotional challenges of childhood. This predisposes them to feel even more helpless and vulnerable as they experience normal parenting procedures.

It is a human tendency to see reality through the victim mentality, rather than look for middle ground. When I first began to work as a therapist, I took at face value whatever a client expressed as the facts of a situation. In subsequent sessions with the friends or spouses of these individuals, I began to hear completely different versions of the "facts." Now I understand that each individual has his own unique "take" on what he sees and experiences. Each individual's perception is influenced by past conditioning and determined by subjective impressions. A person often sees and experiences his relationship from the opposite pole of his partner, from the point of view of how he is being maligned, opposed, or oppressed, with the true facts of the situation obscured somewhere in the middle, out of sight of all participants.

Physical and sexual abuse certainly do exist, and perhaps are more widespread than we care to believe. I have worked with several men and women for whom the memories of incest are clear and precise, and who did indeed experience incest. I have also seen clients such as Claire who, without clear memory of it, referred frequently to suspicions of having been sexually abused and defined their struggles and failures in those terms. After exploring with them the various memories of childhood, and understanding their emotional conflicts in the present, I suspected in many of these cases that they were looking for a way to account for their emotional problems and perpetuate their attachment to being innocent victims. In working with them, I do not directly debunk their version of reality. Rather, I show how, through their suspicions of abuse, underlying passivity and feelings of victimization can be smuggled in. I expose the emotional investment in defining oneself in terms of the beggar-slave-orphan mentality.

To believe oneself a victim of sexual abuse when it never happened absolves oneself of responsibility for one's negative feelings and life failures. Even if such abuse did occur, one can sabotage oneself by using the memories of the helplessness and betrayal to feed one's emotional attachments and to account for one's difficulty in forging a satisfactory life. Such an individual remains emotionally dependent, easily persuaded by other people's ideas. Stuck in such a passive victim role, autonomous development and self-regulation remain hindered.

I don't want to minimize the effect of bad parenting. It does happen and it affects us profoundly. However, the human tendency to misinterpret situations and react out of proportion to our experiences has not been appreciated. Phobias and paranoia are examples of this tendency we have to elaborate emotionally and irrationally on our experiences.

In more subtle ways, all of us have self-defeating reactions to circumstances and events which trigger our attachments. A couple fights for days because the man misunderstood his wife's comment and felt offended by it, an employee feels criticized by the mildest attempt of a supervisor to improve his performance, and the disappearance of a five-dollar item bothers someone inordinately because he is so quick to feel loss.

As I mentioned, couples describe an argument or conflict between them from completely different perspectives. Each partner embellishes on the feeling of being victimized by the other and each insists that his or her version is correct. Some people in relationships are eager to elicit support from friends or therapists to validate their sense of victimization.

This is why we are so attached to our version of the truth. The "truth" we embrace allows us to maintain our conviction of being innocently victimized and absolves us from taking responsibility for our own behaviors, feelings, and hidden motives. To see the truth is to see that we are "into" feeling neglected, undervalued, unappreciated, gypped, and abandoned, feelings we experience toward ourselves. But when we refuse to see our emotional investment in maintaining negative emotions, we feel more helpless, depressed, unable to regulate, and susceptible to sabotage.

Once again to examine domestic-violence situations, the abuser usually feels some guilt and remorse after the fact, but he is quick to find justifications for his behavior on the claim that he, in fact, is the true victim. A wife abuser, for instance, is typically an angry injustice collector, convinced that life treats him unfairly and that others are out to take advantage of him. He believes wholeheartedly in the reality of his victimization, and that belief is a catalyst, a form of entitlement, for his abusive behavior toward others. Criminals often feel entitled to the proceeds of robbery and theft as a compensation for the neglect they experienced in childhood. They usually see themselves as victims of a cold, cruel world that opposes them.

In Santa Fe, a forty-nine-year-old male history teacher, caught with a naked fourteen-year-old female student in his van, said later, "If I do anything with a kid, it's out of compassion and caring." That statement tells us that, in his mind, the true victimization—that of the student—is either incidental or irrelevant. He is preoccupied with *being* the victim, in this case of a system that doesn't understand his brand of love.

In significant degrees, we create our own self-defeating experiences. Then we feel justified in our negative reactions to them. The way we feel about things conforms to our emotional memories of childhood. If plagued by a victim mentality, we are experiencing the consequences of seeing the world from a self-centered perspective through the eyes of our attachments to the three categories of primary emotions—deprival, control, and rejection (described in Chapter 2).

The political correctness movement that surfaced in the 1980's has its roots in the victim mentality. Teachers and professors have been reprimanded and even fired for saying things, typically of a sexual or racial nature, that have offended others. Sometimes the remarks are foolish and insulting, though not necessarily cause for dismissal. Other times they are controversial and provocative in ways that may be useful to jolt students out of their passivity or preconceived notions. But many of those who complain, those supporters and sympathizers of the political correctness movement, are not handling well, for emotional reasons, the challenge of having free speech.

A certain family dynamic accounts for their feelings of being offended. In such families, the truth about each other's feelings either was not allowed or, at best, was incidental to the demand for validation and obedience. They were taught to be careful about what they said. As children, they were required to validate Dad's and Mom's self-image and world views. They had to say "the right thing" (whatever pleases) and repress "the wrong thing" (whatever had the potential to offend). Their own truth, what they felt and perceived unadulterated through their own experience, was dismissed as inappropriate or wrong. As children of easily-offended parents, they grew up to be easily offended themselves. They tend to take all words and comments personally, and to identify with those who they imagine might be offended. They become like their parents, casting reproof on anyone who is free to say what they weren't free to say. They sacrifice hard truths to take the rough edges out of our language.

This illustrates how greatly we are influenced by our childhood, and in ways we are unaware of. And when such correlation is pointed out, we often resist seeing it. Thus many individuals who believe in "political correctness" vehemently deny that childhood perceptions have any bearing on their current beliefs. "What I feel is validated by external reality," they proclaim. But their reality consists of the search for opportunities to feel insulted and offended.

Stepping outside the victim mentality also involves seeing

the role of negative messages (and what we interpreted as negative messages) delivered long ago by our parents. One moment we felt ourselves being validated, appreciated, and loved by our parents, and the next moment it seemed that we couldn't do anything right. These parental messages include, "You're not as smart as you think; just consider yourself lucky to get by; I'm about ready to give up on you; no one cares what you think; I can't trust you to do anything right." These messages don't always have to be spoken; they can be implied in the attitudes, expressions, and body language of parents. We absorb these messages and, through the voice of our inner tyrant (the Speaker of Self-Aggression), subject ourselves to them mercilessly.

All of us have a tendency to pick up on the negative, while the positive is taken for granted. These negative impressions of being inadequate and defective sometimes leave the deepest imprints on our psyche. We may love our parents and feel how much they support us and wish us well, while nonetheless their worst features and messages live on in the cruel and sarcastic admonishments we direct at ourselves. From that place within ourselves we are bombarded with verbal attacks not only for our alleged misbehaviors but also against our very substance and essence. This self-aggression is perhaps the worst form of victimization and, when externalized as it always is, it becomes the model or basis for how victimization is experienced and created in the world.

The negative messages of parents are not accurate assessments of their children, but represent instead the parents' projections of their own self-doubt, their own affinities for feeling criticism and even self-hatred. Unable to screen out the distortions contained in these attacks, the child weaves these parental messages into a direct assault on himself, resulting in a victim mentality. It is so important for parents to gain insight into their own insecurities to avoid the unconscious temptation to dump their insecurities and self-doubts onto their children.

We understand better our beggar-slave-orphan mentality when we correlate our current emotional attachments and negative attitudes toward ourselves with the emotional sensitivities of our childhood. Many people ask, "Why study my childhood? The past is past, and has no relevance for me now." This is pure and simple denial. Even worse, this stubborn refusal to consider the power of the unconscious is a form of stupidity because this willful ignorance causes so much personal suffering and is hazardous to the future of the human race.

The unconscious mind doesn't distinguish between new experiences and emotional memories from the past. We draw on a stockpile of past experiences—and the emotional interpretations we gave to those experiences—to evaluate each new situation. So we react to present reality through past experiences and beliefs. This is one of the most elementary principles of psychology, and to deny it is as foolish as insisting that the world is flat.

Becoming self-responsible and acquiring self-mastery is a learning process that involves moving away from childish beliefs and feelings into adult maturity and wisdom. It means learning and understanding the motivations and intent behind our feelings and behaviors. Inner freedom is the state in which we see reality outside the beggar-slave-orphan mentality, as co-creation and interaction, involving our participation in shaping events. It involves learning how to avoid personalizing reality in order to see it as refusing us, constraining us, or freezing us out.

When this knowledge and consciousness are assimilated, we will achieve a fundamental reformation of character, a realignment of purpose, a renaissance of values, and unification with our true self.

CHAPTER 6

Sabotage in the Workplace

When I worked as a journalist years ago, inner accusations of my faults and shortcomings reverberated down my pipes, into my organs, and rattled my bones. My experience of myself was too amorphous and so I wasn't aware of these subliminal accusations. I just felt anxious and fearful, defective and unworthy. I felt a lot better when I produced good stories and thereby "proved" my value to my co-workers and to myself.

As I now can see, much of my energy was enlisted, not to write good stories for newspaper readers, but in an inner operation conducted by my *unconscious ego*, to neutralize inner accusations of my unworthiness. This unconscious ego of ours is a kind of inner Central Intelligence Agency that devises and manages our defenses, strikes compromises with our inner tyrant, and covers up the truth of our collusion in misery and self-sabotage. When my creativity stalled, along with the flow of "headline" ideas and stories, my unconscious ego faltered in its attempts to defend me against the tyrant's attacks, knocking my anxiety off the charts to become irrational fears of being fired. Sometimes I became depressed and apathetic and fell into deep slumps that boosted my misery average and lowered my work performance.

Why was I suffering like that? I was a decent, hard-working fellow. Why couldn't I accept myself as I was? Clearly I was at war with myself—and apparently on the losing side. I understood this conflict and began to resolve it after getting some answers about the nature of the psyche.

In addition to our self-image, we all have an idealized image of who we are and who we expect to become. But I was failing to live up to that idealized image. (Idealized image is different from self-image. Self-image is more conscious, an accumulation of impressions of who we are, while our idealized image is not consciously recognized.)

This idealized image is the *ego ideal,* a self-concept that is formed in early childhood primarily to restore the lost connection with ourselves, our true self. A child is speaking under the influence of his ego ideal when he boasts about what he can and will do in the future: "I'm going to be president when I grow up," or "I'm going to be the greatest artist in the world." Becoming the ideal of what would please our parents and society defends against the loss and hurt of not being loved for who we are, for just being ourselves.

Our ego ideal becomes a serious problem for us, as I am about to explain.

Sigmund Freud discovered the existence of the ego ideal and in his 1914 paper, "On Narcissism: An Introduction," he wrote that what a person "projects before him as his ideal is the substitute for the lost narcissism of his childhood in which he was his own ideal."[1.] (Freud's writings have been under attack for the past several decades. We have a tendency to debunk that which challenges us so we won't feel guilty for, as Joseph Campbell put it, our "refusal of the call." Nothing challenges us more than coming to an inner realization of the value of much of what Freud brought to light.)

Let us set the ego ideal aside for a moment and introduce a major player on our inner battlefield, the harsh inner conscience that I call the inner tyrant. Freud believed the inner tyrant, or superego as he called it, developed when a child, finding that he must of moral necessity renounce the satisfaction of revengeful aggressiveness against the authority (mother) who denies him his sense of himself, finds a way out by identifying with the authority (mother) and directing the aggression onto himself. "The authority," Freud wrote, "now turns into the superego and enters into possession of all the aggressiveness which a child would have liked to exercise against it" (the authority).[2.] Later, Edmund Bergler stated in his book, *The Superego,* published in 1952, that the superego is the hidden master of the personality and the seat of self-aggression. Because of the superego, he wrote, "Man's inhumanity to man is equaled only by man's inhumanity to himself."[3.]

Unlike our healthy conscience that is an aspect of our essential goodness and is aligned with what is wise, this harsh conscience indeed acts like an inner tyrant. Fueled by the aggressive drive now directed at ourselves, it strikes out at us with vicious, trumped-up charges, using as its model of reproach an exaggeration of those parental messages that we felt as controlling, criticizing, and rejecting.

How is it possible, you ask, that such a tyrant could lurk inside us? The following is Bergler's elaboration (briefly stated in Chapter 2) on the explanation first put forward by Freud. We are all born with natural aggression, which is a survival instinct. But there exists a peculiar flaw in our engineering: our young musculature is too weak to expel this substantial aggression outward, especially when aggression boils over due to feelings of being trapped in helplessness and powerlessness. Despite a baby's attempts to expel the aggression, which culminate in crying, screaming, and furious temper tantrums, much of the aggression is nonetheless "introjected" or turned inward where it contributes to the formation of the inner tyrant. A condition is then established in all of us in which we become the object of our own aggression.

The aggressive drive is like a river; it has to flow. Once it has been directed at ourselves, it can flow as easily against us as outwardly toward others or external challenges. It comes at us in the form of self-rejection, self-criticism, self-disapproval, self-mockery, self-condemnation, and self-hatred. Usually we don't see that these feelings are then projected onto others and the outside world. Inwardly, we are on the receiving end of an intense persecution by a subliminal battery of accusations, an inner vindictiveness that accounts for why people tend to be so self-critical and defensive.

This self-aggression is a primary cause for a person's stubborn emotional conviction (much different from an objective, intellectual assessment) that he is inadequate and unworthy. Thus we are sensitive to criticism and disapproval from others because that is what we are doing to ourselves. In other words, we buy into self-negating messages from others because those messages represent the inner tyrant's accusations which mirror what we are secretly ready to believe about ourselves. Meanwhile, we torment ourselves imagining that others see us as flawed and defective, or that they hardly notice us because we are unworthy of being noticed.

We may in our hearts be proponents of nonviolence, but on the psychic battlefield our tyrant attacks, often quite viciously, and we defend, often quite ineffectively. The tyrant eagerly lashes out at us with any discrepancies found to exist between the grandiose presumptions of the ego ideal ("I am great; I will do great things") and the hard-nosed reality of our less-than-glamorous circumstances in the world. We feel guilt, anxiety, and intense dissatisfaction when reminded inwardly that we are not living up to our ego ideal and the expectations we place on ourselves.

My reality as an ordinary journalist didn't correspond with my ego ideal, which stubbornly held to the illusion that I was not only very important but extraordinarily talented. As punishment for not living up to my ego ideal, my tyrant launched a covert verbal assault—"Ha! You thought you were going to be so great! Now it's obvious you'll never be good enough and never amount to anything! And that's what you really want, isn't it—to feel that who you are and what you have to offer doesn't matter to anyone!" I didn't actually hear those words, though I am sure their decibel level was over one hundred. All I did was react to the effect of them.

It mattered for naught that my ego ideal was an infantile illusion concocted to cope with the loss of my true self. My tyrant has only one function—to find a target or a direction of flow for its aggression. Thus, a Department of Self-Aggression, as sympathetic to my life and liberty as a rabid terrorist, usurped a corner of my mind and set up headquarters. For years I suffered in a self-contained, existential misery, unaware of this covert operation. In recent years my understanding of the existence of my self-aggression has become a shield that deflects much of its sting. The flow of self-aggression has itself abated in the process of working out my attachment to the feelings of self-reproach and self-condemnation.

We see our self-sabotage more clearly when we understand that our inner program of self-criticism and self-negation takes precedence over success and happiness. In fact, it is important that success *not* be attained, that we remain blocked in our creativity and self-expression, and preoccupied with our inadequacies, so that the program of self-criticism, fueled by all this continuing evidence of our shortcomings, can flourish. All that matters to this impersonal agenda is the continuing operation of the established program.

Once we understand that the self-aggression emanating from the inner tyrant consists mostly of "empty words," or invalid and exaggerated accusations (the slightest misdemeanor is proclaimed a felony), we no longer take the words and accusations to heart. On an inner level, we are now able to neutralize or deflect these accusations. Eventually, the accusations themselves can become muted.

Our self-aggression appears to some like a diabolical force, interested only in our suffering and defeat. Another view is to regard it as an energy configuration similar to an electric current, totally indifferent to its effects. My preference is to give it an evolutionary value, to see it as a force for good that is intended to prod us out of our unconsciousness, forcing us through its incessant agitation either to suffer its effects or to awaken through its prodding to greater intelligence, compassion, and love for ourselves, and to a fuller appreciation of the splendor of who we truly are.

Under the exposure of our awareness, the harsh inner tyrant loses its influence. As we become more conscious of its existence and purpose, it no longer has the same disruptive power. In the process of realizing this inner opposition, we gaze beyond our self-centeredness, through the protective screening around our self-image, to see our true self shining at our side. As we discharge the hateful energy of the inner tyrant, we are at last fully free to create peace within ourselves and in the world.

Breaking the Shackles

You may know a person who is in an unsatisfactory position because he doesn't think he deserves better, or a friend who loses jobs because he provokes his bosses, or an acquaintance who is easily discouraged and quickly gives up. Perhaps it is you.

Many of us are capable of considerable achievement and may also be brilliant, but end up shackled to forms of self-sabotage. Our jobs and our workplace environments represent a replay, with new characters, of the leftover emotional conflicts from our childhood experiences. As young adults, many of us head off into the world of work with fear of failure. Often, as the hidden motivation behind the pursuit of success, we are trying to prove that we are *not* failures. Unfortunately, before long we are often establishing as our reality the deeply held conviction that indeed we are.

Fear of failure translates into our expectation of failure, which further translates into the likelihood that failure, at least in one aspect of our lives such as career or relationships, will be acted out. The expectation is present within us because, emotionally and unconsciously, we regard ourselves as inadequate, inept, and undeserving. If we are ensnared in these feelings and beliefs about ourselves, we indeed become a failure (or feel like one) in our personal lives, our careers, or both.

Your first step to addressing a dismal track record with work or career is to see whether you are blaming others, extenuating circumstances, or yourself. If you are blaming yourself, you are likely doing so for the wrong reasons. For instance, you may think you are having trouble in your career because you are lazy, don't have a showman's personality, aren't smart enough, assertive enough, or focused enough. But nine times out of ten these are claims to power—all secondary, not primary, problems. You may be a job-hopper, a low risk-taker, a work-shirker, a dead-end jobber, or a get-rich-quick schemer. Underneath all of these surface symptoms are our emotional attachments and our secret willingness to play the game of self-sabotage.

The adult who feels he has been a disappointment to his parents often acts out what is called a *negative pseudo-moral connotation*. This is a defense through which, unconsciously, the person abdicates responsibility for his life and weakens his self-regulation. The negative pseudo-moral connotation, in its bitter sarcasm, goes like this: "You see, Mom and Dad, I've become a failure, just as you expected. But I'm not responsible for what's happening to me. I'm only being what *you* expected, what *you* thought I'd be, what *you* really wanted me to be!"

Clearly, we see how important it is to clear out left-over feelings toward our parents and resolve our interpretation of the messages we received from them. In part, our left-over feelings are due to our own propensity in childhood to take on negative impressions of our parents' intentions, actions, and interventions. We need to see our attachment to these negative feelings and impressions, and see how we use it against ourselves. Whether our parents were culpable or not is no longer the issue. What matters now is our attachment to whatever negative emotions and impressions we have absorbed.

The adult using such a negative pseudo-moral as a defense is likely to pass an emotional curse along to his children, for he will see and hate in his children the disappointment and sense of failure that he hates in himself. His children will assimilate the same feelings of disappointment because, when all remains unconscious, we absorb coming at us from our parents what they soaked up from their parents.

In the following example, a client of mine, a lawyer named Robert, displayed an assortment of emotional characteristics that contributed to his failures. Robert came out of law school with all the apparent ingredients to rise to the top in his profession. He had posted high grades, was intelligent and articulate, and appeared to be motivated to excel. Although Robert worked hard, the law firm he had started three years earlier was almost bankrupt.

Depressed, in a panic, and convinced he was a hopeless failure, he began to explore with me the subtle emotional issues that were sabotaging him. Although Robert knew intellectually he had good potential, deep down he felt inadequate. He didn't really believe in himself. At business functions or social events, he observed himself being awkward and shy. He sensed that others saw him as defective and even unworthy.

We explored his passivity and lack of confidence. Robert was letting people take advantage of him; he had failed to establish boundaries, and he was catering to his clients in ways that left him feeling bad about himself.

"Maybe I'm just too nice," he suggested.

"You're a good person," I replied, "but you have some emotional quirks that we'll expose and help you overcome."

Criticism and rejection were familiar feelings from Robert's childhood. As an adult, he tended repeatedly to experience and even provoke these negative feelings from others. Because he wasn't performing adequately in his work, his wife had to step in to compensate for what he didn't earn. In her eyes, he didn't meet his responsibilities, prompting her to be critical of him. Robert's partner felt the same way and had made plans to leave the firm.

If his self-sabotage remained unconscious, Robert would indeed act out being a failure, the pathetic object of disapproval and reproach. His emotional problems can only be understood in the context of his childhood, as is true for us all. His father, an accountant, hadn't felt fulfilled in his career. Robert's mother had a strong personality and held the family together. But his father went from job to job, feeling like a failure. That feeling was reinforced by Robert's mother who didn't respect her husband and nagged at him for not promoting himself and being more successful.

Robert felt abandoned emotionally by his father who seldom praised or encouraged him. His mother, meanwhile, pushed Robert to be perfect, as if she wanted him to make up for his father's weakness. Robert went off to law school, anxious to please his mother, but unconsciously identifying with his father and receptive to his father's inner feelings of self-rejection and self-disapproval. Unfortunately, these conflicts compelled him to act out an agenda in which he replayed with others the emotional drama his parents had scripted.

As Robert gained insight into what had previously been unconscious, he began to understand the nature of his passivity and self-rejection. The primary understanding involved his growing awareness that he was unconsciously attached to feeling rejected and disapproved of, as a result of the rejection and disapproval he directed at himself. The lawyer in him needed proof that these emotional attachments were the culprit, and the proof consisted of his understanding of the many ways he provoked rejection and disapproval in numerous daily incidents when he failed to respond appropriately to challenges or made poor choices. He knew from previous experience that he could conduct himself with grace and poise. So his bumbling and stumbling could only be negative exhibitionism, the result of his propensity to believe that he was responsible through his ineptness for the failure in his life (rather than to see the true cause in his self-disapproval and his use of failure to affirm his self-rejection.)

Robert had worried that a female client was unhappy with him. He had made a few minor mistakes in this person's paperwork. These had been corrected before any harm was done, but he had overreacted emotionally to his errors, brooding for days, drinking more than usual, and lying awake at night with visions of his clients gossiping about his faults and failures.

I taught him a technique for regulating these emotions. "When you're caught in an emotional predicament such as this," I said, "you want to expose the self-sabotage going on beneath the surface. You can say to yourself, 'This feeling of disapproval must be what I want. This is how I see myself. I disapprove of myself in so many ways, just like I felt it in childhood, remembering how it was for my dad, identifying with what he was feeling about himself, about mom's attitude to him, and how he was viewed by his colleagues.'

"You also need to be aware," I continued, "that your inner conscience will attack you with the very same words of criticism and disapproval that your mother directed at your father and that your father felt toward himself. You can observe, as a consequence, how you feel defensive much of the time. Watch how you defend yourself. Observe these inner processes as a witness, taking note of the irrationality of it all."

I added, "Whenever you expose the negative way you regard

and treat yourself, you begin to moderate or regulate your reaction. You are making an inner correction or adjustment that enables you to experience your situation more appropriately."

Through this technique, Robert realized more deeply the extent of his secret willingness to disapprove of himself and imagine others disapproving of him. In observing his reactions, he began to catch himself defending himself. These defensive thoughts of his ("I'm trying my best; I'm under a lot of stress; I'm going to be more attentive") were in themselves evidence that he was under an inner attack for his alleged inadequacies.

"You don't have to answer to this inner prosecutor," I told him again. "His allegations are, at best, petty misdemeanors and most often completely false. Yet you react as if you're being accused of felonies. You want to keep an eye on this harsh inner tyrant and know what his game is, or automatically you'll get caught up in defending yourself."

"It's true," he told me once, "I must be attached to rejection and disapproval. It's the only explanation to account for them being such themes in my life. It's the only explanation I can think of. I know it's more powerful than just a bad habit. Bad habits I can break. This is more. Some part of me is determined to subject myself to these negative feelings. It's kind of scary and it's hard to believe. It's incredible, actually! But as I accept this, I have never felt in a stronger position to turn my life around."

He did become stronger, others responded favorably to him, and he saved his law practice and his marriage.

Robert's primary emotional problem had been his attachment to feelings of rejection and disapproval, and his readiness to *transfer* these onto others in order to maintain and reinforce the feelings. Transference, as I have said, is our unconscious compulsion to experience repeatedly the emotional memories from our past through present situations and relationships. Transference is a common cause of personality clashes, marital discord, and conflicts with supervisors, clients, and co-workers. For instance, bosses often become father figures, meaning that the emotional issues that existed between an individual and his or her father (such as feelings of being criticized or rejected) are transferred onto a boss. Now the boss is the one viewed as being critical and rejecting. Of course, bosses and co-workers can also become "mother figures," and now the unresolved issues and accompanying emotions that transpired between a mother and her child are repeated years later by the grown adult in his or her relations with men, women, and children.

As mentioned, we are inclined to dismiss the concept of transference, preferring instead to believe that the negative feelings and reactions we experience are caused by the insensitivity or malice of others or the hardships of life. This belief that others or difficult circumstances are to blame for our problems maintains the feelings of being helpless and victimized or leads to inappropriate retaliation and aggression. Once transference is understood and recognized, we are able to see more clearly how we sabotage ourselves.

Our Passivity Works Overtime

Many of us never advance in our personal lives or careers because we feel controlled and dominated by supervisors, bosses, and co-workers. The requirement of work in itself is often taken as an offense. Work was first introduced to us as a duty, a concept that contradicts the childish notion that "I can do whatever I want." Americans spend billions on lottery tickets in the dream of winning and thereby doing nothing for the rest of their lives. The workplace has become hell to millions of us because we ourselves experience it emotionally as a place where we are deprived, drained, restricted, controlled, demoted, and otherwise oppressed.

In varying degrees, we felt dominated in childhood. We were

forced to submit to the will of someone else, initially our parents. Toddlers first experience control during early childhood socialization and toilet training, and the tantrums of the "terrible twos" are their way of rebelling against the feeling of being forced to comply with someone else's agenda. Some of us adjust better than others, making appropriate emotional and rational compromises to accommodate this experience.

I used to feel exceedingly controlled in work situations, like a slave chained to my desk, watching in helpless agony as the clock ticked toward quitting time. I had felt controlled and intimidated by my forceful mother, forced to do the chores she set aside for me, required to comply with her point of view, and obliged to accommodate her interpretation of what it meant to be a male. I felt corrected and bossed around—told emphatically how to wash dishes, fold clothes, make my bed, hang the bathroom towels, use a knife and fork. Not only was I expected to do it her way but exhorted to be enthusiastic in the process.

To avoid feeling completely swallowed up by her, I resisted passive-aggressively—doing tasks carelessly, leaving jackets hanging on door-knobs and the cap off the toothpaste tube. I felt I couldn't possibly win against her; the only power I had was to fail to meet her expectations of me and thus to frustrate her. I remember how much I hated the feeling of being passive to her, and how I hated myself for being hopelessly mired in that passivity.

For years after joining the work force, I felt controlled when asked to work overtime or perform a work function that wasn't included in my job description. I often sat in the office working on tasks of my choosing rather than do what supervisors wanted done. To respond wholeheartedly to a request from them left me feeling extremely passive. To cover up my attachment to feeling controlled, I claimed through my defense, "They can't make me do anything! I'll do what I want!" I had no idea of my secret propensity to exacerbate feelings of being controlled and oppressed. Even when my supervisors reacted with annoyance to my feisty non-cooperation, I believed that my defiance was in my best interests, reflecting my autonomy and ambition.

Sometimes we believe that our negative feelings and reactions toward work are justified by our boss's insensitive behavior or by the overwhelming requirements of the job. A client with this problem asked me, "What am I supposed to do when I experience my stressful, blatantly unfair job situation—just lay back and say nothing?"

"Before you decide what to do," I answered. "it's more important to be clear *why you feel the way you do*. Are you seeing all the elements in why you're feeling so oppressed at work? In your situation, you create your own passivity, meaning you bring upon yourself the impression of being acted upon by others and you feel yourself to be oppressed by your boss and by circumstances. Your situation is challenging but not oppressive. For emotional reasons, however, you experience it as oppressive. The more you catch yourself in the act of creating that impression and holding on to it, the sooner you'll dispel that unpleasant impression. True, your boss may be insensitive and unwise. Nonetheless, you have your emotional involvement in the conflict, so you have to see what you bring to the table from your own past."

Some of us feel controlled simply by life's daily requirements. We view having to work and support ourselves as something we are forced to do, rather than a fulfilling life challenge. Low productivity and lack of creativity can be a result, caused by conscious or unconscious rebellion against this feeling of being forced and restricted. The emotional conflicts waste our energy, leaving us depleted, and give us, we feel, even more justification for our grievances. Sometimes we feel controlled or oppressed even in ideal work environments.

Often we rebel against our parents' high expectations for us because we feel so controlled by those expectations. Thus, unconsciously, we defeat ourselves in order *not* to feel controlled and defeated by others, initially our parents. To succeed feels like giving in to someone else's expectations and requirements. Or, in order to hold our parents accountable for our failures, we may secretly feel, "If I succeed, that lets mom and dad off the hook. It means they weren't such bad parents after all."

The problem, of course, is not with our parents or others but with our own propensity to take on feelings of being passive and controlled. Signs of this type of passivity in the workplace include:

* Frequent confrontations with authority figures; feeling bossed, pushed around, or forced to submit;

* Strong urges to get away from the office or fantasies of quitting; frequent daydreaming;

* Difficulty making decisions and passively letting others infringe on one's delegated authority;

* Missing deadlines, coming to work late, and procrastinating as a passive-aggressive reaction to feeling forced or dominated;

* Feeling sorry for oneself and feeling that the world is unfair;

* Not being motivated with work and career because of feelings of powerlessness and helplessness;

* An inability to be firm with clients and customers.

Other Ways to Sabotage Ourselves

Missing the Boat. Another way we torment ourselves is through the feeling of missing the boat. This experience is a consequence of indulging in feeling deprived and refused. Signs of this emotional difficulty include high levels of impatience, frequent dissatisfaction, and the inability or unwillingness to commit to our endeavors or projects and carry them through to completion. We always have excuses for our dissatisfaction, such as claims that our job is going nowhere, that we are not being adequately rewarded, or that we are not appreciated. But usually our problems are deeper than that.

The preoccupation with missing the boat sometimes compels us to try to make things happen quickly, other times to procrastinate. Behind our anxiety is the emotional conviction that not much good will occur in our lives, that we are not meant for success, that whatever we produce will be discounted or ignored. Consequently, we become our own worst critics, lack motivation and purpose, and experience all efforts as unpleasant.

When we expose this emotional aspect—that is, our secret willingness to cultivate the feeling of missing out—our feelings and perspectives change dramatically. It is like facing your enemy in the light where he can be defeated, instead of in the dark where you can't see what you are up against.

Procrastinators. Procrastinating is a way we passively resist our highest good. Procrastinators have different emotional reasons for their passivity. One may be a perfectionist ready to find fault with whatever he tries to accomplish. To cover up his affinity for feeling criticized, he does nothing. But he can't win—now he criticizes himself for accomplishing nothing or for not living up to his potential.

Another procrastinator holds back because he feels that he is being forced or pushed into taking care of the tasks at hand. Instead of enjoying the work, he feels that he is submitting to someone else's will or agenda, or that he is helpless and overwhelmed by life's requirements. His procrastination, then, becomes a passive-aggressive reaction to the feeling of being forced to submit to authority or situations that require his compliance. Procrastination may also cover up fear of success, as happens when we procrastinate to block our advancement because we feel we don't deserve success. Or we may feel passive to the many demands and responsibilities that success will require of us.

Other procrastinators are plagued by ambivalence. As soon as they try to move in one direction, they begin to doubt themselves, wondering whether another procedure or method is preferable. If they shift to that alternate course of action, they begin to doubt that choice too. They carry within an emotional conviction that whatever they try to do, whatever choices they make, aren't going to work. Inner messages of self-doubt—"Are you really sure you're doing the right thing?"—are less harsh than self-criticism and self-reproach but can still sabotage us.

Some of us make little progress because we are convinced we will never match the accomplishments of our parents. The main blocks, in this case, are our tendencies to compare ourselves unfavorably to others and to keep ourselves in a passivity which consists of our inner willingness to harbor feelings of being inadequate.

Workaholics. These individuals are compulsively dedicated to work. They sacrifice their health, pleasure, and the love of family members because they are so desperate to neutralize inner accusations of their unworthiness. They use work to prove their worth. Take away what they do for a living and they feel empty, as if they have no substance.

Thus, the workaholic is likely to be dependent on flattering approval from co-workers, supervisors, and others. Even after an exhausting twelve-hour day, he may continue to be absorbed with business worries and doubts about his performance. Meanwhile, he looks down with scorn on those he feels don't share his ambition or zeal for work. He does this because he sees his own weakness and failure in them. To counteract the accusation of his own lack of value, the workaholic, in projection, scorns or strikes down the perceived weakling.

As a defense, workaholics sometimes employ a *pseudo-moral connotation* (as opposed to the *negative pseudo-moral connotation* mentioned earlier in this chapter) which goes like this: "There's no ulterior motive for my hard work. What I'm doing is appropriate. Didn't my mom and dad always tell me it's important to work hard to get ahead?" The pseudo-moral represents the misuse of an educational precept, cunningly misinterpreted to sanction a deviation of the original command, to one's ultimate detriment.

Lacking Creative Expression. Negative messages from the past about our capabilities can block our creative spirit. I remember feeling humiliated in my first year of high school when, in front of the class, the assistant principal snorted with derision at a picture I had drawn. Subsequent trepidation dogged my every attempt at art. Artists abide in my family and I'm sure, given time and training, I could have excelled.

So fear of failure blocks creativity. We are afraid to confirm what we are so ready to believe about ourselves, that we are inadequate and defective and can't excel. We often associate our labors with the very essence of ourselves. With this belief, it is all or nothing: our work is either perfect or it is not good enough. If one's work is rejected, the individual takes it personally: "If my work is not good, then I'm no good." Or we may believe that, "Since I'm no good, I surely can't produce anything worthwhile." Also, when we are evaluated or criticized for performance or behavior, we can be tempted to feel that our whole self is being negated because that is how we treat ourselves.

Even when we are successful, we carry within ourselves an element that devalues our success. One client of mine, an artist, was making more money and acquiring more recognition than he had ever imagined. Yet the pleasure of his success was undermined by his doubts about the continuing flow of his creativity. Despite his success, he still bought into inner accusations of his flaws and inadequacies. In time, he learned to deflect the negative influence of his self-negation, primarily by observing the accusations with objectivity, detachment, and his growing ability to refrain from defending against them. He was finally able to enjoy his success without being nagged by self-doubt.

Not supporting oneself emotionally. We can abandon ourselves, or betray ourselves, even as success eagerly reaches out to be embraced. This is more likely to happen when we have had parents who we feel were not supportive and withheld attention and love. If they didn't acknowledge our qualities, and didn't let us know in word and deed that they believed in us, we can be left with a deficiency of confidence and self-trust. We will overlook ourselves and our finer aspects, thereby doing to ourselves what we felt was done to us.

Or we may reverse this and overrate our abilities, which can also be self-sabotaging. Parents sometimes exaggerate their child's abilities, though in their body language, tone of voice, facial expression, and innuendo they exude doubts of future success. We grow up and overrate our abilities because we lack emotional certainty and expression to confirm our value. We are first in line to undermine ourselves because we are prepared, especially when the stakes are high, to reactivate the old feeling that we are going to be a disappointment to others and seen as not having what it takes to live up to our billing.

Suffering for nothing. We need to watch out for our willingness to take on some form of suffering (headaches, anxiety, worry) in the attempt to "prove" that we are truly sincere about wanting to succeed, prove our worth, or feel fulfilled. The ironic consequence is that we create more pain and suffering to make it look as if we are trying to avoid pain and suffering. For instance, Jack, a golfer, persistently "chokes" or fails to perform at his best in competition, much to his chagrin and embarrassment. When Jack was younger, his father often praised his golf skills, but Jack felt that beneath his father's words was the expectation his son would never do very well. "Too bad you don't get enough time to practice more," his father often remarked after Jack had lost a match.

In Jack's unconscious, he is under an inner accusation that he is emotionally attached to the feeling of losing, that he secretly "gets off" on the old unresolved feeling of looking bad in the eyes of his father and others. "No!" Jack says in his unconscious defense. "I want to look good and be seen as a winner. I'm trying my best. Look how anxious I get before a match. And if I lose as a result of playing badly, I really feel bad. Surely that proves how much I want to win." Unfortunately, all it proves is how much Jack is willing to use anxiety and shame to cover up and thus maintain his unconscious attachment to the feeling of looking bad and being seen as a loser.

Finally, a word about middle-age crisis, particularly as it affects men. When we reach our forties and fifties, still struggling in careers and relationships, we see time running out and realize we may never achieve the goals of youth. Even for someone who has raised a family and held a good job, the feeling is, "Is this all life has in store for me?" Now we are ready to sabotage our chance to live at peace with ourselves in old age. The inner tyrant rushes into the breach: "You see, you loser, you didn't make it! Too bad—if you'd tried harder, you probably could have made it. It's too late for you now, you're all washed up!"

We are reluctant to consider in this middle-age predicament that we are the ones who hold ourselves back and berate ourselves mercilessly. So we blame the one who is closest to us— our partner. How do we know our partner is to blame? Because she is boring and she is getting old. She hasn't lived up to expectations; she has been a disappointment to us. We project onto our partner the disappointment we feel in ourselves, and we may convince ourselves that another partner is just the tonic to restore our vigor and our purpose.

Some middle-aged rebels—again, mostly men—go through with plans to become involved with another partner, often a younger woman in order to "prove" they are still young and attractive. Others retreat into discontent, passivity, and hypochondria, postponing all plans for a renewal on life. In either case, the current partner is blamed for the rebel's discontent.

If you believe your partner has let you down, consider taking a good look at yourself. What you are feeling about your partner is a direct reflection of what you are feeling about yourself.

Work-History Profile and Exercises

This work-history profile and other exercises are designed to help you take responsibility for a lack of success in your career or for the feeling that work is a dreary necessity. It may take two or three hours, or longer, to answer these questions thoughtfully, so take some quiet time in order to collect the information. Or else do only fifteen or twenty minutes of writing at a time. Keep your notes and answers in a notebook or journal so you can review them frequently as you look for more understanding of your limiting patterns. Some questions may appear to be repetitious, but I ask similar questions in different contexts to help you come up with new thoughts and feelings and to generate insight.

a) Write down all the major jobs you have held. For each job answer the following questions:

* What motivated you to take this job (career)? What did you hope to gain? Include emotional gains.
* What did you like about this job?
* Describe your positive skills or talents in this job.
* Describe your weaknesses in this job.
* What did you not like about the job?
* What feelings were triggered in you by this job?

* How did you get along with your boss and co-workers? Describe any interaction issues. How did you feel around them?

* Why did you leave this job or change your career?

* Did you work at your highest potential with this job?

b) Look over all of your jobs. Pull out the common themes, feelings, or patterns that seem to persist. For example, boredom, anxiety, too skilled for the job, feelings of inadequacy, and so on.

c) Describe your parents' work history. How did each parent feel about his and her job? Were they happy or discontented?

* Do you see any parallels between your work history and your parents' work history?

* How did your parents define success?

* Describe any negative messages that you may have received from your parents, either directly or indirectly, about your skills and ability to perform.

d) Describe your present situation with regard to your work or career.

* How are you feeling about it?

* Do these feelings correlate with the feelings and patterns in your work-history profile?

* Do you feel this way about other areas of your life, such as your relationships with others or with yourself?

e) If you are not happy with your present situation, describe your fantasy of what you would like to be doing. If you could have any job in the world (no matter how unrealistic it may sound) what would that be? Why do you want this kind of career? What will it give you? If, for example, you say you want to help people or want to make money, why is that important to you?

* Describe your present relationships with your boss and co-workers. What feelings come up for you? Do they relate to similar feelings with parents or spouse? Do you feel controlled, criticized, or disapproved of?

f) What are the reasons you give yourself for not doing what you want? Ask yourself, "If I attempt to do what I really want, what will happen or what is stopping me?"

* Who or what do you blame for your lack of success or confidence?

* List any fears you have with respect to your job or desired career.

* What are your negative expectations?

* Trace each fear back to childhood and come up with a memory that depicts this fear. (It might be at school, at home, or both.)

* List all the negative things you tell yourself about your skills and strengths. What reasons do you use to account for why you don't succeed or earn more money?

g) Talk about what it means to value yourself, to believe in yourself. Where does lack of confidence come from?

Write up an itinerary of all the things you do well. They don't have to be work related, e.g., you cook well, throw good parties, or are personable, decisive, humorous, precise. (If we don't value ourselves, we can't value these everyday strengths. Consequently, we don't draw upon these resources or don't include them in a resume. You must project a belief in yourself, the feeling that you have value. To do that you must define precisely the inner accusations that convince you otherwise.)

h) Imagine yourself successful in some venture, such as sales, an artistic endeavor, community service, and so on.

Describe this success in detail. In other words, list the criteria that determine this success. For example: 1) Do you work for yourself or do you have employees? 2) How much money do you make? Are you aware of a certain boundary with respect to how much money you earn? 3) How do other people regard you?

* Close your eyes. How does success feel? What are the positive aspects? What are the negative aspects? (If you can't define success specifically, it might not happen. You have to see it unfolding before you, step-by-step. You need a blueprint.) Can you allow yourself to feel successful?

* What negative thoughts or feelings come up for you when you imagine success? Do you have any fears or negative expectations, such as, "There's no time for myself; others will depend on me; others will feel abandoned?"

* If you are a woman, are there negative connotations to being a successful woman, such as fear that you would become selfish, hard, or not feminine? Finish the sentence: "Successful women are…"

* What excuses do you give yourself about not feeling successful? List the ways you sabotage your goals.

* What are the negative messages you give yourself about this successful scenario? How do you discount and discourage yourself from getting on with your aspirations?

* What are the origins of these negative messages? Who in your past or present are you allowing to discourage you? What were your parents' messages regarding success? What were their expectations of you? Describe their successes. How did they feel about themselves and their ability to become successful?

* How much money do you want? Why did you choose that amount? Is this how you value yourself? How do you feel about your present money situation? Describe your historical relationship to money. What does it mean to you? Describe your parents' feelings about money and what money meant to them.

In summary, most people don't realize the extent of their negative attitudes and their negative treatment of themselves. But we can see it all around us, for this negativity is reflected in our interactions with others, in the situations of our lives, and in the collective. Everything we experience is a reflection of how we feel about ourselves.

CHAPTER 7

Mastering Inner Dynamics

Let us delve into the archives of psychological literature to consider the works of Dr. Edmund Bergler, a psychoanalyst and prolific writer who died in New York City in 1962. We are looking for more understanding of the nature of this inner negativity.

Bergler's theories, first put forward more than sixty years ago, are the foundation on which I have written this book and form the basis of my understanding of self-sabotage. He maintained that an unconscious part of ourselves is attached or addicted to negative emotions. We develop these emotional attachments in childhood and bring them forward into our adult lives. These attachments, unconsciously maintained and elaborated on, are the cause of the emotional and behavioral reactions that constitute self-defeat and self-sabotage.

Bergler gave us a comprehensive framework for understanding our emotions and for learning to regulate them. He wrote twenty-two psychology books and 273 published articles, and a 400-word obituary was written about him in *The New York Times*. A Jew, he fled Austria in 1938 to escape the Nazis and he established a private practice in New York City. In Vienna he had served on the staff of the Psychoanalytic Freud Clinic from 1927 to 1937.

Some of his best-read books include *The Writer and Psychoanalysis* (based on the analyses of thirty-six writers) and *Money and Emotional Conflicts,* both published by Doubleday; *Divorce Won't Help, The Basic Neurosis,* and *Conflict in Marriage,* all published by Harper and Brothers; and *Tensions Can be Reduced to Nuisances,* published by Collier Books. He wrote for professional journals such as *The Psychoanalytic Review, Diseases of the Nervous System, Medical Record, Journal of Clinical Psychopathology, Quarterly Review of Psychiatry and Neurology, International Record of Medicine, Western Journal of Surgery, Obstetrics and Gynecology* (on frigidity in women), and the *Archives of Criminal Psychodynamics.* (Many of his books are in print and available from International Universities Press in Madison, CT.)

He also wrote for popular magazines such as *Cosmopolitan, Coronet, Charm Magazine, Pocket Book Magazine,* and *Harper's Bazaar.* Titles of articles he wrote for these publications include: "A Psychoanalyst's Case for Monogamy," "A Psychoanalyst Looks at Fashion," "Reduce Your Tensions to Nuisances," "The Hoax of the He-Man," "There's No Magic in Psychiatry," and "The Type, 'Mr. Stuffed Shirt.'"

Yet we have completely resisted a full reflection and ongoing study of Bergler's theories. Doctoral graduates in psychology come out of American universities without even having heard of him. Not a mention is made of him in Morton Hunt's *The Story of Psychology* (1993), nor in Peter Giovacchini's *A Narrative Textbook of Psychoanalysis* (1987), though both books discuss the contributions of scores of lesser lights.

Bergler was, in my opinion, the greatest researcher into *orality,* a term which refers to the consciousness of the child in the first eighteen months of life. The most deeply buried memories of our experience as humans come from the oral stage.

Sigmund Freud, who had published his first book before Bergler was born, was in a sense the first archeologist at the site. He investigated human experience closer to the surface, first the oedipal or genital stage (experienced from ages three to five) and, deeper and to a lesser degree, the anal stage (experienced from 18 months to three years). Freud never penetrated in any detail into an understanding of the human experience of the oral stage. Of course, it is predictable that he would discover the more recent layers of development closer to the surface.

Bergler acknowledged Freud's intellectual achievement, and it became the foundation he required to go deeper into the mystery of the psyche. Bergler became convinced that the oral period constitutes the major influence on one's emotional health. He also believed the child's experience of his external situation—parents, siblings, family members, home life—is not as influential as his biologically-determined inner experience, meaning how a child assimilates and accommodates the conditions of his childhood through his own unique emotional nature. In essence, Bergler wrote, our emotional health and growth rest in large measure on how successfully in the first few years of life we accommodate the affronts to our primal egocentricity as we are faced with reality factors.

Bergler, painfully aware of the enormous resistance to his ideas, once said his books were time-bombs that would go off in 100 years. Perhaps now, faced with intensifying disruptive forces in the world, we can speed up the timetable.

He wrote that we are *neurotic* (an out-of-favor word that has been supplanted by *dysfunctional)* when inner conflicts impede us from enjoying our work, block us from compassion and love, and prevent us from enjoying hobbies and social interests. In the conclusion of *Divorce Won't Help,* published in 1948, he wrote, "The outlook for licking neurosis is even more optimistic in the United States than in Europe. The great vitality of the people, their energy in fighting dangers once they are understood, and the great resources of the country make it more than likely that the problem of neurosis will be solved, as many other problems have been."[1.]

According to Bergler, our emotional nature has a life of its own within our unconscious mind and is greatly influenced by what he called *psychic masochism.* Psychic masochism should not be confused with perversion masochism, he wrote in 1954. "Perversion masochism…is present in merely negligible quantities in the human race," he wrote in *The Revolt of the Middle-Aged Man.* In contrast, "psychic masochism, while still largely an unknown disease, is one of the most widespread of human failings. To define it briefly, it is the unconscious wish to defeat one's conscious aims, and to enjoy that self-constructed defeat." It is much more comforting, he added, to view oneself as a victim than to admit "that one is an unconscious seeker of defeats, humiliation, kicks."[2.]

Bergler wrote that psychic masochism was humanity's greatest secret and greatest curse. This masochism consists of unconscious attachments to negative emotions such as refusal, control, and rejection (representing the three categories of primary emotions listed in Chapter 2). Any pleasure or satisfaction from this masochism is very seldom recorded consciously. Occasionally, individuals may be slightly aware that their melancholy holds some allure and that their self-pity and injustice collecting have a bittersweet taste.

Any masochistic pleasure that is experienced unconsciously, and which we are often driven to experience through compulsions, obsessions, phobias, and addictions, is paid for a hundredfold in conscious guilt, envy, anger, anxiety, depression, fear, and other forms of suffering.

Can this be true? How jarring it is to our sense of reality! What does it mean? We would not have buried Bergler and his books so deeply in the recent past, and thus repressed this knowledge of our own developmental origins, were this knowledge untrue. We bury the truth of ourselves deep within ourselves. Thus, logically, we will bury it wherever it arises, in this case in the archives of psychoanalytic literature. The consignment of Bergler to the ash-heap of history has not been a conscious plot. It has been the outcome of humanity's massive resistance to inner truth and self-realization. Our resistance is indeed incredible; were some readers to agree intellectually with this theory of masochism, their emotional aversion to assimilating it would nonetheless remain steadfast. As the truth of our massive deficiency of self-awareness draws near, a feeling like the bile of revulsion swells in our throats.

In the light then of the theory of psychic masochism, what I have been calling emotional *attachments* can also be considered as emotional *addictions*. And what I have been referring to as passivity, as described in Chapter 4, is the painful and ineffectual condition of being caught in the masochism while unconsciously tolerating its effects. Self-sabotage, in the numerous ways it is acted out, is a direct consequence of this need for the negative.

Despite our best intentions, we are consistently pulled back into the vortex of our negative emotions. If we begin to see that the magnetic pull enticing us into negativity is, in fact, masochism, it is like having a shovel instead of a plastic teaspoon to get to the roots of self-sabotage. Knowing it is masochism, and catching ourselves in the act of engaging in it, we can say, "Now I see the game! Now I know what I'm dealing with! Now I can feel that this isn't going to get the best of me!"

In connecting this masochism with the operation of the inner tyrant, Bergler said that the self-aggression dished out by the inner tyrant is *libidinized* (sugar-coated or made addictive), meaning we transform the self-aggression into an experience of masochism as a trade-off to protect our sense of power. This masochism originates in the first months of life when the baby deduces, in his primitive egocentricity, that he must want whatever he is feeling: "Whatever happens to me, even if it doesn't feel good, is what *I* want and what *I* seek." This reflects his inability to distinguish himself as separate from outer reality.

The term *psychic masochism* was not introduced sooner in

this book because I have observed that many people simply can't deal with it. It sends shudders down our spine and many of us close off completely to its implications. To this point I have used the euphemism *emotional* or *secret attachments*, gradually leading readers to a place of possible acceptance of our psychic situation. In my practice, my clients seem better able to access their masochism by first processing it as emotional or secret attachments.

An individual comes into a *knowing* of this inner situation as he processes the knowledge through painful childhood memories, his self-depreciating attitudes and behaviors, and the meaning of his defenses, reactions, and patterns of self-defeat. Consequently, he begins to experience himself making positive shifts in his relationship to himself, others, and the world.

Evidence of our masochism can be see in the degree to which many of us "buy into" the inner taunts, accusations, and mocking sarcasm that we direct at ourselves. We are constantly defending against these verbal assaults or trying to neutralize them, even as we know intellectually they are unwarranted and invalid. This is why we often feel badly about ourselves, or believe others see us in a negative light, despite knowing intellectually we are basically good people trying our best.

Bergler wrote in the conclusion of *Principles of Self-Damage*, published in 1959, that the "majority of analysts avoid as unpalatable the fact that psychic masochism is universal; they show even more distaste for the fact behind this fact—the unremitting cruelty of the superego. But science cannot be converted to the program of happy endings adhered to by the slick magazines. Even distasteful facts must be swallowed when their accuracy has been demonstrated."[3.]

Freud began to suspect the important influence of masochism. Though he first published his discovery of the superego in 1923, he later became more aware of its cruelty and irrationality. He wrote in 1932 that the superego had chosen only the harshness and severity of our parents, and not their loving side, with which to address us. In *Civilization and Its Discontents,* a short book published in 1930, Freud wrote that undischarged infantile aggression accumulates in the superego and then is directed back against the individual as self-aggression. He also wrote in a discussion of what he called the *death instinct,* that "I know that in sadism and masochism we have always seen before us manifestations of the destructive instinct (directed outwards and inwards), strongly alloyed with eroticism, but I can no longer understand how we can have overlooked the ubiquity of non-erotic aggressiveness and destructiveness and can have failed to give it its due place in our interpretation of life."[4.]

As early as 1920 in *Beyond the Pleasure Principle,* Freud began to sense that, contrary to his earlier beliefs, masochism did perhaps contaminate the psyche. He wrote, "Masochism, the turning around of the instinct upon the subject's own ego, would in that case be a return to an earlier phase of the instinct's history, a regression. The account that was formerly given of masochism requires emendation as being too sweeping in one respect: there *might* be such a thing as primary masochism—a possibility which I had contested at that time."[5.] Freud's observations on the central role of masochism weren't followed up by other researchers (other than Bergler), and in fact his thoughts on the subject were attributed by many to a waning of his intellectual powers in old age.

If Bergler and Freud are right, as I believe, this is one of the deepest, darkest, and most liberating secrets of our human nature. It certainly explains why the lack of self-regulation and its self-defeating consequences are so agonizingly persistent in our personal lives and in the world. It certainly affects all our relationships. How can we feel close to others when we harbor expectations of being seen by them as defective or inadequate? How can we feel close to ourselves when we are attached to doubt, disapproval, and criticism? How can we be receptive to God's love when we harbor a secret program for feeling deprived, neglected, abandoned, and unloved?

I believe we can achieve a dramatic renewal as individuals and society if we can have the courage to understand and take responsibility for this aspect of ourselves. Since the human potential movement blossomed in the 1960's, many have engaged in a personal odyssey to become more aware of the meaning of their behaviors and feelings. Yet despite this effort, many of us remain stuck in old patterns. Some individuals who have persistently endeavored to improve themselves within certain psychological systems feel frustrated by their lack of progress and refer in quiet despair to "the limitations of awareness." And many progressive individuals themselves are riddled with issues and conflicts concerning self-doubt, self-rejection, and self-hate.

Many of us feel that, "I know what my problem is, but I still can't seem to change my feelings and behaviors to get beyond it." I contend, however, that people don't know what their problem is if they are unaware of the nature of resistance, the clever stratagems of our defenses, our appetite for the masochistic experience of ourselves and life, and the self-aggression underlying it all. Obviously, our masochism and especially our defenses against it can be quite subtle and difficult to identify. But nonetheless this knowledge, I believe, represents a new psychological "technology," an instrument for the 21st Century to move through our resistance into growth, transformation, and reunion with our true self.

The chronometer, discovered in the 1700's by the Englishman John Harrison, represented a dazzling breakthrough for human intelligence. It determined longitude and thereby the ability to position oneself on the great expanse of the high seas.

What we need now is a technology in the form of an unassailable truth to position ourselves in relationship to ourselves, to each other, and to all of life.

Finding such a point of reference in the vastness of inner space seems to many to be a monumental undertaking. Our defenses are determined that such knowledge remain beyond our reach, mainly to protect the illusion of the ego's supremacy and to maintain the balance of power in the unconscious. Bergler wrote in *The Writer and Psychoanalysis* that the fight for a good life is waged both within and without, and it is the inner battleground "that complicates the life of the individual to a point which simple 'common sense' can scarcely comprehend, let alone accept."[6.]

Let us look again at self-sabotage. The following few examples of masochism and self-sabotage have been simplified to help our understanding. On the surface, a jealous person hates to be rejected or betrayed, but his unconscious masochism consists of his attachment to those very feelings. Thus, his jealously is the result of his own self-rejection and self-betrayal projected onto others, though he claims earnestly that his fear of rejection is valid and supported by external factors. Consciously, the jealousy is painful to him. In experiencing the pain of real or potential betrayal, he acts out the pain of his own self-betrayal. "No, not true that I reject myself," he proclaims in his unconscious defense. "I'm not looking to feel betrayed! Can't you see how much I hate that feeling!"

The jealous person's secret *wish* is to feel betrayed, a wish that reflects back to him his self-negation. Thus he often brings about the very thing that he secretly wishes for. This illustrates the nature of masochism—what we say we hate is what we secretly wish for and, as it relates to the inner rejection of ourselves, results in acting out of self-sabotage in our daily lives.

A perfectionist hates to be criticized. He tries to do everything perfectly. But consider how harshly he criticizes himself or how he imagines others are criticizing him when he does some little thing wrong. His secret wish is to feel criticized, reflecting his own inner critic. A person with this secret wish is likely to become a perfectionist and suffer the agonies of both this impossible calling and the constant experience, from within or outside himself, of feeling criticized.

A procrastinator hates to feel pressured and controlled. But it is secretly what he wishes for. The more he procrastinates, the more pressured and controlled he feels by the duties or obligations he is procrastinating against. It is agonizing for him, yet he goes on procrastinating because, unconsciously and emotionally, he is under a compulsion to enhance the experience of feeling controlled. He also procrastinates so that secretly he can berate himself and condemn himself for not being productive and living up to his potential.

A promiscuous person is attached to feeling unloved. The promiscuity is a search for some form of love, and the desperate yearning for love serves as a defense to make it appear that the person really does want love, when all along the wish is to feel unloved. Here the great lack of love is for oneself. The chronically lonely—"Nobody loves me, nobody cares"—are also indulging in the feeling of being unloved, unwanted, and abandoned.

The workaholic is desperately trying to validate himself in order to gain appreciation and self-approval. But beneath his compulsion to work, he is attached to inner criticism that he is unworthy and has no value. The workaholic is also interested in using work to distract himself because he comes under more bombardment from his inner tyrant for being defective or worthless when he is at rest or trying to be at ease. Because of the relentless inner attacks to which he is attached, he doesn't know how to be at peace with himself, and so he hides from himself through compulsive activity.

Our masochism comes in three varieties, based on the three categories of negative emotions involving deprival, control, and rejection, as outlined in Chapter 2. All three are obfuscated by hundreds of dynamic, shifting defenses and thousands of forms of self-sabotage. Sometimes the three categories of masochism all come together around one expression of self-sabotage. For instance, an individual's compulsive overeating can be held in place by feelings of deprival, control, and rejection.

When you are masochistically attached to feeling, say, criticized, you may feel you are being criticized even when you are not. You will criticize yourself, sometimes mercilessly. You will provoke feelings of criticism by being careless, apathetic, or insensitive, inducing others to disapprove of you. You will also go where you can find and act out your attachment, such as teaming up with a partner who has a strong tendency to be critical. We become living pin-cushions for what we are attached to. Meanwhile, through it all we hate the feeling of being criticized and we may hate those we feel are critical of us, a reflection of our self-hatred.

As a general principle, whatever you are afraid of, or especially sensitive to, is what you are masochistically attached to. If you are sensitive to feeling criticized, that is your masochism. If you are sensitive to rejection, then that is your masochism. And so on. Through defenses such as blaming, excuses, transference, and projection, as well as many varieties of behavior, we try to cover up our masochism. Often, we resort to the claim-to-power defense through which we blame ourselves for the wrong reasons (i.e. being lazy, dull, selfish, or lacking in character or personality), rather than recognize our problems are being caused by the underlying masochism.

When we are masochistically attached to feeling controlled, we may get angry or apathetic, lose our will to succeed and prosper, get in fights with our wife or boss, feel like giving up on our life, or come under the controlling influence of people, ideologies, or substances. If we are addicted to rejection, we may feel jealous, lonely, and unworthy, and act out by driving our loved one into the arms of someone else, or eat and drink too much. There are many combinations and permutations of possible self-sabotage based on the underlying masochism.

Dramatic change is possible. Our masochism can be neutralized. It may take some time to achieve this completely, but as we begin to study ourselves in the light of this knowledge we can feel the stirring of a new ability to moderate our reactions, to regulate our feelings and behaviors, and to determine our destiny.

The current popular acceptance of pharmaceutical drugs for emotional health constitutes a major resistance to seeing the truth of our human nature. Sometimes, in certain circumstances, tranquilizers and mood stabilizers are appropriate as a temporary measure. It is very seductive to give in passively to a drug or some external agent in an attempt to correct our imbalance. In contrast, unlocking the secrets of our emotional nature can force us, propel us, into higher intelligence as we understand ourselves more fully and become more powerful and loving. If we settle for drugs, we will lose so much of what makes us human—our intelligence, our dignity, our integrity, even our freedom. We certainly won't address or change the masochism that makes us our own worst enemy. It may be that pharmaceuticals, as well as illicit drugs, have taken such a hold in our society because of our unwillingness to take responsibility for our inner conflicts and because of our infantile dependency on an outside source to make us feel better. This plays into the hands of the inner tyrant which (who?) remains unchallenged.

Three Lessons in Identifying Our Masochism

Each of us has periods of self-doubt, when we wonder if we are good enough, times we feel as if we don't belong, times we feel helpless to improve our situation. The cartoon character Charlie Brown rings true because we all know what it means to feel helpless, hopeless, and inadequate. To some degree, most of us are hampered, and often impaired, by these feelings. Even when we know intellectually that we are good people, the emotional conviction of being inadequate or defective (created, maintained, and reinforced by our masochism) can become our reality.

Sometimes we are so convinced we are defective that we seek to punish ourselves. Marie, a former drug user and bulimic who had been shy and withdrawn since childhood, described these feelings to me: "I just couldn't be condemning enough of myself. All my destructive behaviors were a way to demolish myself, to punish myself for being defective, ugly, and repulsive. I felt so loathsome that even death was too good for me. My suffering was the only appropriate punishment."

Painful as it was, Marie had been firmly entrenched in this impaired sense of herself and couldn't imagine life without this identity. "I knew it would be the death of me if I stayed that way," she said, "but I also felt I would die if I was any other way."

She was right. It would feel like death to reverse her plight; she would die to her old identity and be reborn anew, experiencing herself without her masochism. Were this deliverance from her inner plight to happen overnight, she might feel disoriented, like a political prisoner rushing blindly into the night from her escape tunnel. As it happens, the process of inner liberation is usually gradual. We are more likely to be complaining it is occurring too slowly.

I proposed a path of personal growth in my book, *See Your Way To Self-Esteem*. This book describes how the *emotional imagination*, or what psychoanalysis calls the *visual drive*, can be usurped by the unconscious mind for self-defeating purposes, generating irrational fears and self-limiting feelings. In fact, the emotional imagination is fueled by our masochism and our self-hatred. The challenge is to expose the inner structure whereby we allow the emotional imagination to be used in wasteful speculation about our prospects, painful reflections on the past, and truly harmful considerations about our lack of worth and likelihood of failure.

The following three lessons reveal more about the art of self-responsibility and self-regulation. Learning self-responsibility isn't so much a matter of *doing* something positive as a process of *undoing* what has been set in place within us, while seeing more clearly into our emotional investment in maintaining our self-negation and our resistance to loving ourselves. The garden grows of its own accord once the weeds are pulled away.

Self-responsibility involves the deepening capacity for self-observation, which means learning to monitor ourselves objectively and being a witness to what we are experiencing. We enrich our experiences by being simultaneously aware of being a participant and an observer. Often people are at one extreme or the other—the shy person is all the observer (in the subjective, self-absorbed sense) and feels cut off from the pleasures of participation, while the gregarious extrovert may be all participation, with little reflection on his impulses and motivations. The following three lessons are designed to help us develop and strengthen self-responsibility by becoming more observant of the subtle ways we are willing to entertain and party all night with our self-rejection.

The first lesson involves improper use of the imagination, the second, negative peeping, and the third deals with our receptivity to negative inner voices.

(1) Improper Use of the Imagination

How well do you use your imagination? Writers, artists, scientists, entertainers, and others use their imaginations to create dramatic effects, useful products, or beautiful objects. Another good use of the imagination is to produce pleasant or enjoyable fantasies and to live in tune with ourselves in the present moment. This doesn't mean we should spend a great deal of time daydreaming about an idealized future, a behavior that could signify emotional difficulty accepting life in the present.

Because of our masochistic relationship to ourselves, many of us misuse the imagination and become enmeshed in life-negating thoughts and emotions. Worriers, for example, are always imagining bad things happening in the future. This causes them to suffer with worried feelings in the present moment. Often the things they worry about never occur. All that happens is that they suffer for nothing.

Worriers produce visualizations of bad things happening without being aware of the inner feelings that induce or inspire their negative images. Here is an example of how we do this. A woman who is worried about being overweight is invited to a party. For a week before the party she tortures herself with images of being seen in a negative light when she gets to the party. Yet she goes and has a wonderful time. So she worried and suffered for nothing—except to re-enact how inadequate and defective she feels about herself. In another example, a man says something inappropriate at a business meeting. For the next forty-eight hours he tortures himself with images of how those at the meeting are thinking ill of him (reflecting how he secretly sees himself), although in fact what he said, even though inappropriate, was never held against him and was soon forgotten by the others.

In order to stop producing visualizations that maintain our anxiety, we have to begin to see and understand that we misuse our imaginations to fulfill a secret agenda, that of generating familiar negative feelings about ourselves, which are then projected onto others and life in general. If you find yourself worrying about, for instance, lack of money, say to yourself something to this effect, "In order to suffer for the next two hours,

I'm going to produce a visualization of myself being deprived of money and having to go and beg for it shamefully from my relatives because I see myself as such a loser. This is clearly the feeling I must be wanting to generate."

Tracking our emotional indulgences is challenging because both the fact and the consequence of misusing the imagination often are not conscious. All we feel are symptoms such as depression, withdrawal, anxiety, or fatigue. The man who spoke out inappropriately at the business meeting, for instance, might have experienced depression for several days afterward and not consciously have connected the depression to his *faux pas* at the meeting. Were he to take his awareness to the next level, he would understand that his depression results from the fact that he is still indulging unconsciously in feelings of being criticized by his colleagues, as well as his inner tyrant, for what he said. In recognizing this self-criticism, he is able, in effect, to put it aside or put it in its place, and thus to resist the temptation to continue to indulge in it.

As I said, we often look into the face of another and, instead of seeing the other person objectively in his own right, we see what we feel about ourselves, the sensation of being looked at with rejection or disapproval. We spend a lot of time imagining that others see us as inadequate and unworthy, even as fakes or frauds, because that is how we feel about ourselves. We do not do this consciously. That is why we are quite offended when we see or imagine the anticipated negative reaction coming back at us from the other person. "He's got his nerve," we are apt to say. "Who does he think he is, treating me like that?" This is, of course, our defense—how we avoid seeing our own attachment to seeing ourselves as inadequate or defective.

Through the emotional imagination, we create false impressions of reality. In the example above, we generate the belief that others see us in a negative light or are out to get us somehow. Then, as we begin to act as if the false impression were the reality, we can become the embodiment, through body language, tone of voice, and personality, of someone whom others do indeed see in a negative light (i.e., a braggart, a wimp, a bore, or a jerk). The more we are steeped in self-negation, the more we are apt to engage in *negative exhibitionism* (the acting out of the claim-to-power defense that contends, "*I* cause others to look at me as defective or bad"). Now, as we provoke others, we indeed get to be seen in a negative light, affirming our negative feelings about ourselves. This puts on another layer of defensive protection, to saying nothing of the cost in more painful consequences, over our secret wish to be looked down upon.

Both our will and our capacity for self-responsibility are stymied by the false impressions that we take as reality. The solution is to gather enough insight to see how a part of ourselves is always ready to believe the false impressions. We acquire the knack of catching ourselves in the act of looking for problems that don't exist or magnifying ones that do exist, as we correspondingly expose the part that wants us to believe the worst about ourselves and others. We learn to recognize the self-condemnation that previously operated outside our awareness, thus bringing it into our conscious life and weakening its influence.

Exercise

Try this exercise in inner watchfulness to catch yourself producing negative scenarios. Think of something you are concerned about, something that bothers you. Maybe it is a problem in the family, a spat with a friend, or maybe you are worried about a problem at work.

Ask yourself, "How much time do I spend every day producing this scene and the feelings that go with it? What is the feeling that I get into with this scene? Do I feel bad about myself? Do I feel sorry for myself? Do I blame my feelings on others? Am I acting out what I felt with my parents and being a disappointment now to myself and others? Do I criticize myself? Do I see myself failing, or being rejected? Am I feeling lonely, abandoned, controlled, or criticized?"

As you do this, can you detect within yourself some tendency to *indulge* in feelings of being unloved, unwanted, a disappointment, or seen as inadequate or defective? Is this how you see yourself?

Now, imagine that you are able *to catch yourself* in the act of producing (in your imagination) scenes or images of bad things happening to you. When you catch yourself in the act of producing negative images, you can begin to see how you are misusing your imagination. You also understand your reason for doing so, which is your attachment to the negative emotion that you conjure up through this misuse of your imagination. You realize how you thus contribute to your own fears, anxieties, dissatisfactions and, ultimately, self-sabotage.

As I have said, it is crucial to see and understand the reasons we allow the misuse of our imagination (or abdicate responsibility for putting it to better use). When you do see this, you understand exactly what you are doing that is self-defeating and thus you can choose to respond appropriately. Now it will be easier to believe in yourself, to see a bright future for yourself, and to orient your imagination and your will in a way that helps you move in a positive direction.

(2) The Thrill of Negative Peeping

Lesson number two involves growing in awareness of how we use our eyes (as opposed to our imagination in the previous lesson) to see things that reinforce negativity and low self-esteem. We call this *negative peeping*.

Millions of us roam the earth with hungry eyes, a part of our unconscious mind on alert for evidence that we are being unfairly treated. Instead of using our eyes to see beauty or to experience enjoyment in the present moment, we are looking for ways to recreate familiar feelings from our past of injustice, neglect, and deprivation. We may be doing this if we are avid readers of fashion and celebrity magazines or fans of *Lifestyles of the Rich and Famous.* Then we are like pretenders to the throne, *coveting* what we are emotionally invested in *not* obtaining or what is beyond our reach. We are also peeping when we compare ourselves or judge others in order to feel either inferior or superior to them.

Let us say that Brian, a boy with low self-esteem, is convinced emotionally that he is disliked by a group of fellow students. If he is a negative peeper, he will subtly spend time at school watching intently for evidence that others really do dislike him. Those other students, however, may not be thinking about him at all. But Brian, through his self-centeredness, is either convinced they are, or he is convinced they ignore him because (1) they are insensitive and mean-spirited and (2) he is unworthy of their attention (claim to power). Either way, he is on the lookout to catch them in the act of rejecting or ignoring him.

If it were true that the other students did indeed dislike Brian, he could be provoking their dislike through negative exhibitionism, which in Brian's case would be his unconscious compulsion to act out his attachment to being seen in a negative light. For instance, he might act out being a "geek" or a "nerd" when being that way is not at all who or what he really is.

As a negative exhibitionist he could indeed say as a defense, "I'm not looking for the feeling of being rejected. It really does happen. They don't want me; they actively reject me because I'm clumsy and awkward." But now, to maintain this defense, he has to really believe in his alleged defectiveness.

His negative acting-out is self-sabotage and is a consequence of his emotional attachment to the feeling of being rejected. Brian can become aware of his secret attachment to rejection by catching himself in the act of negative peeping, meaning he would begin to observe himself actively looking at situations involving the other students for the purpose of generating within himself feelings of being rejected or excluded.

This is the cause-and-effect mentality in action. Brian believes he feels bad because he is rejected, when all along he is co-creator of the situation. He feels bad because of his self-rejection, not because the students are making him feel that way. Through his eyes, he cultivates feelings of being rejected, overlooked, excluded, and seen as having no value.

Meanwhile, in his self-centeredness, he sees the world only in terms of how he sees himself; consequently, he believes that what he sees relates to him. He sees the world *subjectively* rather than *objectively*. His impressions have little to do with reality and more to do with his inner conflicts and his experience of himself.

When you look at the world, how do you feel? Do you see others getting more than you? Do you see people who are indifferent to your existence? One example of negative peeping is the child who watches closely to see whether his brothers and sisters get more love from Mom and Dad than he does. In his unconscious, he is using his eyes to feast on the feeling of being deprived or unloved. A peeper is someone who walks around the office, while his eyes absorb others being more popular or more privileged than he. When he does this, he is using his eyes, unconsciously, to feed feelings of being overlooked and unimportant, which is precisely how he feels about himself.

The trick is (1) to become aware of this unconscious compulsion to look for the negative in yourself and in life; (2) to recognize the specific negative self-depreciation that you feed on; and (3) to identify your resistance to seeing the good in yourself, in others, in nature, and in your life. Your eyes serve you best when you see the wonder of things, how amazing life is, and how much there is to be grateful for.

(3) Critical Inner Voices or Feelings

Lesson number three involves the battle of the inner conscience, the struggle to neutralize the inner tyrant. As I have described earlier, we are all plagued with critical inner voices and feelings. These critical voices (or subtle negative feelings) can leave people convinced that, "No matter what I do, it's never good enough."

These voices or unpleasant feelings of self-doubt, self-reproach, and self-condemnation constitute self-aggression. Through these inner voices and feelings we often make accusations against ourselves that are worse than anyone else would ever make. The voices represent a negative caricature of our parents, in which the commands and requirements they directed our way in the process of raising us are rendered in the extreme. As mentioned, this system of "inner torture" is set up before the age of three when we believed that our parents' dictums, commands, and requirements *are what we ourselves want and have asked for.* We internalize the voices of our parents, and we end up repeating to ourselves those old maxims and reproaches—intensified in the negative—long after we have left home or our parents are dead.

You can learn *not* to buy into the message of these voices. To do this, you need to see the voices for what they are, like random charges of electricity that are set off because of quirks or bugs in your internal operating system. More specifically, you become aware of how you feel about yourself, how you resist thinking positively about yourself, how you mistrust, abuse, and neglect yourself, and how you avoid measures that would promote your highest good.

Sometimes the inner voices or feelings are unconscious and so quiet you don't know what is happening. All you know is that you are depressed or anxious. It is hard to figure out what is going on. You have to become a detective in your own psyche, and listen to yourself and observe your feelings.

As a tip, observe your mind's contents to see what it is you are defending against with your thoughts and feelings. Several years ago I caught myself defending against my choice of four new tires. I bought them at a tire outlet that was close to home but didn't carry the brand of tires I would have preferred. The new tires, I thought, didn't ride quite right on the road, so I went back to the tire shop and left my vehicle for a test ride. Later, the attendant who tested the car said that, without a doubt, the new tires were just fine. Nevertheless, I continued to feel irritated and anxious, even after accepting intellectually that the tires were all right and that I would keep them. While I didn't perceive the inner accusations at that time, I realized later that I had been "hitting myself up" with inner thoughts and feelings, to the effect that: "Look at you, you jerk, you paid too much for the tires! You allowed yourself to be taken in by their sales pitch. To return them now would make you look like some idiot who doesn't know what he wants."

I was clearly under an accusation of paying too much for them and being passive with the store manager. Once I figured out the inner accusations and remembered my emotional willingness to take on such feelings of doubt and criticism, I could see what I was doing to myself, using this situation as another opportunity to put myself down. Soon I was feeling fine again. The tires transported me safely and were no longer an emotional problem.

Inner voices were nagging a man I once met for lunch at a restaurant. As we walked outside after eating, we approached his old, somewhat battered Oldsmobile. Suddenly making his car the focus of attention, he piped up: "It's not new but it's got a new motor in it. You wouldn't believe how well it still drives. Hey, cars are way too expensive nowadays. I'm going to get my money's worth out of this baby. Besides, I need to save enough to play golf."

The man was entertaining the feeling that I would judge him according to the value of his automobile. He must have imagined I was thinking: "Look at this car, it's a worthless pile of junk. What kind of person would drive an old junk-heap like this?" This man saw himself as a worthless piece of junk and thus transferred onto me the expectation I would see him that way.

Exercise

Try this procedure for deflecting inner voices. What is it your inner voice has said to you recently that left you feeling bad about yourself? This is tricky. If you can't come up with anything directly, try to imagine what you commonly criticize yourself for. Maybe you made a mistake at the office, and for days or even weeks you have nagged at yourself for it. Maybe you said something you regretted to a friend or an acquaintance and inwardly you are being nagged at for being stupid or foolish.

Imagine you are sitting in a movie theater. The critical words of your inner voice are being projected onto the movie screen, and you can see the words as they pass across the screen. Watch the words. Now, monitor yourself. Are you feeling criticized? Are you prompted to defend yourself? Are you tempted to play down the significance of the words? Don't try to stop the words or thoughts or even judge them. Just watch them.

Imagine what it feels like *not* to defend, *not* to react, but simply to be present to yourself. Can you go into yourself, to a place of knowing that the words are empty and malicious, and that there is no need for you to be defensive or reactive? Simply see what you are doing to yourself. How does it feel to be on the receiving end of such a barrage?

The critical words or feelings can be deflected or neutralized instead of piercing you in the heart. You just need to be aware that the words or feelings constitute impersonal self-aggression picked up in your past and which have nothing to do with who you truly are. Emotionally, out of ignorance you have been willing to absorb them, regardless of whether the accusations are valid.

Many of us identify with our minds. And so we don't separate ourselves consciously from the messages or thoughts produced by our minds. This is a consequence of being disconnected from our feelings and ourselves. We are much more than our minds and much more than what our minds produce.

Create a distance, a separation, from your thoughts. Then allow your wisdom to develop as you see which thoughts and messages have value and which ones don't. Especially watch out for those wicked incantations from the inner tyrant that are nothing more than concoctions of self-doubt, self-reproach, and self-condemnation.

Now you are taking responsibility for what you think, for what you believe, and for how you feel. You see more clearly where your thoughts come from, and thus you can discriminate among idle speculation, desires, dissatisfactions, self-aggression, and genuine creativity. Your experience of yourself is becoming crystallized.

CHAPTER 8

Elements of Social Unrest

I see in the newspaper that Charlie Brown has again lost the opening game of the baseball season. Our bald and awkward cartoon friend embodies the worthless feeling in us all. Every day Charlie's sense of unworthiness is confirmed for him in the eyes of others because that is the game he plays best. Though he seems to be apologizing for his very existence, nobody hates him. In fact, we all love him—we know exactly how he feels.

This feeling that we are nobody special, that we are losers more than winners, is an emotional undercurrent that greatly influences us personally, socially, and politically. Feelings of being powerless and insignificant may be more onerous and challenging than ever before. We live in an age of emotional deregulation in which people don't feel as needed as they once did. Modern technology can make us feel obsolete in the workplace. Our labors seem less crucial, less valued, as semi-skilled, skilled, and professional workers are being fired and laid off in government and corporate "downsizing."

Meanwhile, the media play up the exploits of the culture's "heroes," providing us with daily opportunities to compare ourselves unfavorably to others. We glorify winners and celebrities as a defense, to identify with the feeling of being "number one" in order to boost our own self-image and to prove that we are not secretly enmeshed in feeling insignificant. While we identify with the winner and get a boost on what he feels, we condemn losers to ignominy, as we do in politics and sports, and thereby deny and cover up our emotional alignment with that feeling in ourselves.

The media exalt celebrities and ignore the everyday heroes, those who are humble and dedicated to things greater than themselves, because everyday heroes don't seem newsworthy. We love to rub shoulders with a celebrity so we can be recognized by someone upon whom we bestow so much power and glory, compensating for our lack of inner recognition.

Meanwhile, pervasive advertising, which plays up on our tendency to feel dissatisfied and unimportant, separates society into winners (those who partake of the good life) and losers (those who can't afford to). Either you drive a fancy car or you are not as good as those who do. Advertisers get big-name celebrities to talk up cars, cereals, and running shoes. "Be like me, do what I tell you, be a winner instead of a loser," we hear them say between the lines. It is easy to feel devalued when you can't buy into the expensive glamorous lifestyle that is advertising's idea of heaven on earth. We become daydreamers of riches, glamour, and celebrity. Or we become frustrated and angry in feeling deprived and neglected, and conclude that we are either incapable and unworthy of a better life or victims of a greedy, insensitive system.

Marketing and advertising work so effectively at selling us an illusion because we are ready to feel deep down that we are empty, nobody special, and nothing important. Advertising promises escape from this feeling—ways to feel special and important because of what money and the latest products can allegedly do for us. The media mesmerize us with their values—success, celebrity, sensation, self-aggrandizement, and the bizarre—while the advertising and marketing industries dangle the carrot of consumerism and the supposed joys of affluence. We are also tempted to experience feelings of missing out on all the booty and benefits that others appear to have in abundance. We feel we are in competition with our fellow citizens for our share of the "good life." Under this combined influence, we feel devalued and deprived when not partaking fully of these cultural and commercial values.

In our search for validation through materialistic gratification, many of us think of ourselves as *consumers* rather than *citizens*. The word consumer implies entitlement, a condition of getting or not getting, and satisfaction and dissatisfaction, while the word citizen carries a connotation of responsibility and community involvement.

It appears now that our emphasis on such values is catching up with us. The past three or four decades have seen a growing extravaganza of self-absorption that emphasizes selfishness, economic success, "doing your thing," and looking good. We seem more confused, uncertain, and lost than ever.

Meanwhile, casual sex is acceptable and even encouraged as an expression of personal freedom, while divorce becomes a legitimate way to deal with relationship issues. Cocaine, which exalts our self-image, and marijuana, which also enthralls us with ourselves, are the drugs of choice. The entitlement mentality has flourished under these conditions and the revival of self-gratification has taken a toll on tenderness and love. If adults are so much under these cultural influences, imagine what it means for children. Like adults, they become fascinated with material objects and superficial images of value, overlooking the real value that is experienced in personal harmony, integrity, and truth.

Work becomes important for self-image, status, and money rather than for personal fulfillment and the satisfaction of contributing to society's well-being. We get wrapped up in our careers in a way that generates more anxiety than pleasure, while giving our work more value than our families. I have counseled many individuals who don't want the burden and responsibility of raising a family because their own childhood was so unpleasant and because a family would interfere with a career which they feel represents their best chance to fulfill themselves and to prove their value. They feel that children and even spouses take away their chance to stand out in their own right.

We want things given to us without effort on our part because it all seems so accessible, and we feel like such losers without these trappings of value. We are bombarded with allegations of our unworthiness—ultimately and most painfully from our inner conscience—if we don't adopt and acquire the values that, on the surface, make us look good. Because so many of us have not developed a mature, healthy sense of self, we buy up all the glitter and glamour. Then we are more miserable and feel more like failures because even what we have managed to acquire in objects and accolades doesn't fulfill its promise.

Under the onslaught of materialism, advertising, and the breakdown of community, we appear to be embracing self-centered gratification as the primary source of fulfillment. This blocks us from a higher source of happiness, knowing the goodness and divinity of our own unique being.

Connecting the Personal and the Social

In the following overview of various social situations, my intent is to show how, by employing the same psychological principles that apply on a personal level, social conflict can be understood more deeply, thereby improving the chances of achieving social harmony. We enhance our cohesiveness as a people and improve the odds for wise policy decisions when we see more precisely how the individual's emotional patterns become an expression of the collective.

This psychological slant on social situations (and on history as well) says that our personal qualities and shortcomings are also those of the society and the nation. We co-create the society we live in. We are not separate from what is going on around us. The corruption we see in politics and business is the corruption we carry in ourselves. Society comes back at us with all the flaws we contribute to it. When we are dissatisfied with ourselves, or preoccupied with what we don't have or what others aren't doing for us, the collective is soaking in the same feelings. When we are angry at a neighbor and refuse to talk to him, our society remains fragmented and hostile. When we are self-centered and self-preoccupied, society is cold and lacking in civility, business lacks in dedication to quality and service, the arts and media are indifferent to promotion of higher values, and government leaders are more self-serving than nation-serving.

At the same time, we not only give government its legitimate authority, we maintain a parent-child model of interaction with it. We transfer parental authority onto the institution of government and its leaders because we remain attached to (and thus ready to act out) unresolved childhood feelings of being deprived, controlled, neglected, and helpless. Then we protest when the government reacts like a parent, becoming what we feel to be too controlling and intrusive. At the same time we become angry that the government apparently isn't taking better care of us and is withholding from us our daily entitlements. But the government is not a parent and it can't save us from ourselves.

Emotional undercurrents are the basis of nationalism. Our nation is home to many a pseudo-patriot who has transformed his inflated self-importance into national conceit. His self-importance is a consequence of his underlying emotional uncertainty about his significance as a person. If his country is perceived to be strong, this individual infers that he too is strong. If in his mind his country is the best in the world, he recognizes this emotionally as a tribute to his own person. A similar mechanism operates when a person becomes an associate of a powerful individual and uses that union to bolster his own self-importance.

Of course, there is nothing wrong with having powerful stirring of national pride. When a countryman stands on the Olympic podium while the national anthem plays, our inner stirrings of pride and pleasure are appropriate. When national esteem is healthy, we are also remembering and honoring the citizens past and present who have struggled to create and enhance our democracy, prosperity, and respect for each other. But pseudo-patriotism arises from an inner hunger, the felt need to belong to something bigger and more grand than ourselves in order to compensate for how insignificant and unworthy we feel on our own. Any subsequent superior posturing becomes, on a grand scale, petty nationalism.

Since the pseudo-patriot identifies with the nation, he feels flawed and defective whenever flaws are identified in the government or culture. He feels that such criticism is a hostile act made with malicious intent. That is because he himself is emotionally attached to feeling criticized and thus takes criticism personally and reacts to it with indignation. Though the nation's democratic processes need vigilant self-scrutiny, he turns a blind eye to social or political flaws and corruption, just as he is blind to his inner corruption.

Another form of "patriotism" involves Americans who say they love their country but either hate their government or the authorities in the public realm. In this decade, a "madder-than-hell" crowd of everyday whiners and complainers, whose hidden motivation is to sow dissension in order to validate their negative projections, have besieged the nation's airwaves. These individuals are convinced that their outrage is validated by the malice and incompetence of others, when in fact that outrage is simply their means of transferring or projecting outward the conflict and turmoil roiling within themselves. They project their inner discord into the environment and often are passionate and clever enough to persuade themselves and others that their grievances are legitimate.

A healthy person is able to distinguish genuine grievances from what would otherwise be his own transference or projection. Should he chose to address these grievances, he is guided by his strength, wisdom, and compassion.

Some so-called patriots create a world-view that accommodates their conflict-ridden psyches. They establish their intellectual and emotional foundation through the conspiracies they see, the grudges they hold, and the oppression they feel. The last thing they want is peace in the world because that would hold them accountable for their own lack of inner peace.

Some groups in the United States fear that their own government is their worst enemy. Their readiness to resort to violence is evidence of their unconscious willingness to exacerbate the feeling of being oppressed and persecuted. Fringe groups such as white supremacists consist of individuals who interpret their lives through the lens of the victim mentality. On an emotional level, these individuals interpret the government's attempts to curb the proliferation of firearms as a form of control and denial of rights. While the rest of us can understand that such controls are intended to strike a balance for the common good, extremists are unconsciously prepared to exacerbate their negative feelings out of all proportion to the situation. With protests of righteous indignation and various expressions of pseudo-aggression, they are covering up or defending against their masochistic attachment to feelings of being controlled and oppressed. Their pseudo-aggressive reactions such as murder, bombings, and sabotage prompt the authorities to control them even more. Creating the very thing they say they hate is evidence of psychic masochism.

These extremists and domestic terrorists are completely unaware of the degree to which they are in secret pursuit of the feeling of being oppressed. Often they create imaginary oppressors (powerful Jewish bankers, a United Nations-controlled world government) because their unconscious is more interested in creating the sought-after feelings of oppression than in differentiating between what is real and what is imaginary. Meanwhile, they depend emotionally on their guns to compensate for their psychological entanglement in powerlessness and impotence, while their anger and rage are phony exhibitions of strength and power designed to cover up what is really their passivity.

Such fanatical groups usually exhibit a persecution complex, born of their willingness to take on negative feelings of being controlled and oppressed. They have concocted a reality that sees oppressors everywhere because of the degree to which, unconsciously, they are not willing to expose or even consider the lies and delusion that protect their victim mentality. The tyranny they are so determined to see in the outside world is a projection of their own inner tyranny, under which they dance like puppets on a string.

We are all capable of generating irrational fears through the visual drive or the emotional imagination. We entertain feelings and scenarios in which we see ourselves being neglected, abused, deprived, controlled, annihilated, and otherwise victimized. To cover up our own participation in this form of self-suffering, we inflate the dangers and malice presented by outsiders. When we begin to see how and why we create these delusions, we start to take responsibility for our beliefs and feelings by ceasing to manufacture fear.

Even the good guys carry emotional baggage into the social fray. Behind secret intent and hidden motivation are many examples of doing the right thing for the wrong reasons. Someone devoted to helping the poor may be identifying with feelings of deprivation and impoverishment out of an unhealthy attachment to that feeling. *Identification* with the poor or persecuted, be that people or dolphins, is motivated out of a secret willingness to feel deprived, controlled, and cast off as having no value. The healthy person does not *identify* with the neglected or oppressed because to identify with them in their plight means to choose, usually unconsciously, to take on their form of suffering. The healthy person understands the feeling of being victimized and may try to reform a situation out of compassion, or for the sake of justice, or concern for our common well-being. But he does not identify with the victim.

Seeing Deeper Into Our Reactions

Seeing the secret intent and hidden motivations behind our actions is to cast a spotlight on deeper truths. When we don't see deeply enough, we are more likely to engage in futile conflict and to bring out the worst in each other. For instance, an unavailing engagement is being acted out between the gay community and the religious right. Both sides provoke the worst in each other, while secretly reveling in the emotions that are stirred up. The intent here, as elsewhere in this chapter, is not to debunk anyone's beliefs but to understand unconscious dynamics for the sake of conflict resolution.

Members of the religious right feel that the gay community is trying to force them to accept homosexuality as a legitimate and moral lifestyle. However, a secret attraction or intrigue for seeing or imagining what is forbidden, along with an attachment to feelings of helplessness, inclines members of the religious right to give inordinate focus and power to the gay community. This sense of helplessness is based on irrational fears that a homosexual wildfire will render them victims of its "evil" onslaught and scorch them in its wickedness and sin. They also have a secret attraction for peeping, for seeing homosexual acts through their visual drive or emotional imagination, a subtle, forbidden voyeurism that produces anxiety, guilt, and a felt need to condemn what is seen. Usually, this peeping is unconscious. It haunts some members of the religious right because of the inner tug-of-war they create between feelings of being good and being bad. They are tempted to produce fantasies of the alleged evil because its siren song is so alluring to those ensnared in compulsive goodness, a form of goodness designed to protect and promote self-image. When accused by the inner tyrant of indulging in these fantasies, the inner defense contends that the fantasies are necessary in order to appreciate the perversity of the acts. Now, maintenance of the defense requires an expression of indignation and disgust for the alleged perversity. Meanwhile, becoming enthralled with what is "bad" is also tempting to members of the religious right because at the core of their false self they resonate or identify with being sinners.

Meanwhile, gays are tempted to overreact to the feeling of being disapproved of, condemned, and persecuted. Individual gays, as a rule, are emotionally attached to feeling criticized and condemned for who and what they are, and much of their protest against homophobia is a reaction to their own attachment to these feelings and to their own struggle with feelings of self-hatred. Their feeling of being condemned is particularly acute when they identify themselves solely with their sexuality. Individual gays may want to consider, in the battle of the inner conscience, how their inner tyrant can turn on them more viciously than any fire-and-brimstone preacher, assailing them with doubt and negative insinuations about who and what they are. We all doubt ourselves to varying degrees. But for gays who identify with their sexuality, that self-doubt becomes associated with being gay and thus social approval for who and what they are becomes inordinately important to them in their attempt to neutralize their inner disapproval. Meanwhile, when their feelings of being persecuted are processed through a victim mentality, they experience a painful sense of alienation. Self-acceptance and love result from moving toward reconciliation with our true self, a center of consciousness that has nothing to do with sexual orientation.

Psychologically, it is entirely predictable that the members of the religious right, who are inclined to impose their views on others as their elders' views were imposed on them, would react emotionally when others appear to be advancing toward them with contrary views. Adults with a borrowed belief system are on shaky grounds compared with those who feel the truth of their own being through experience and insight.

Should their tenuous belief structure begin to disintegrate, it feels that they will too. Adult children of dogmatic parents can't remember how completely they had to squelch their natural inclination to know reality through their own experience and observation. A sense of helplessness lingers in their emotional nature, often experienced in degrees of paranoia and the fear of being at the mercy of an opposing force.

Throughout history, and notably in medieval Europe when paranoia over the devil was at a peak, religious groups have been obsessed by the prospect of being overpowered by evil. It is a replay of that childhood experience of feeling helpless against what we experienced as some antagonistic force that controls us, makes us submit, and even terrorizes us. The devil's evil, it was perceived, was in part a result of his having a mind of his own. To have a mind of one's own was to oppose God and thus be bad, just as today many groups and individuals consider independent thought and emotional autonomy to be presumptuous. Conveniently, to make the devil image more horrid and their own protection more vital, religious authority "granted" the devil license to seize and punish the willful, the disobedient, and other sinners. Medieval authorities, threatened by displays of autonomy and emotional independence in women, identified them as witches and sentenced them to death.

Some modern witch hunters have succeeded in banning from American schools authors such as John Steinbeck, J.D. Salinger, Judy Blume, and Mark Twain. Such action comes from individuals who weren't trusted in their youth to make decisions for themselves about how the world works. They were told what to believe, how to act, how to think, and how to be. Now they are under an unconscious compulsion to become like their parents and to force their own children, and by extension the community and nation, to submit to this authoritarian model. It feels like betrayal, loss of face, and even annihilation when their children or other adults adopt opposing beliefs. The great challenge for these individuals is to begin to trust their children and others to make independent choices, even though that freedom was not granted them, and to let their children in this new-found openness teach *them* something about freedom, self-expression, and creativity.

Children trigger in us our past childhood parental issues. With our children, we either tend to become just like our parents and treat our children in the same manner our parents treated us, or we overcompensate and do the opposite of what we felt our parents did to us. Both patterns are out of balance and create problems for us and our children.

We can expect as normal, and are wise to tolerate, some degree of opposition, lack of cooperation, and difference of opinion from our children. Children need to have something to oppose in order to become strong, develop their creativity, and become mature and independent. Making your child conform totally to your wishes in this manner sabotages his or her independent functioning. A recent study reported that parents who control their child's food intake to keep him from gaining weight are likely to wind up with a child who doesn't know how to stop eating when he has had enough. The more control the mother reported using, the less self-regulation the child developed or displayed. The study encouraged mothers to allow their children to be more spontaneous about food, that is, to eat only when hungry and not necessarily finish the food presented to them. Children treated in this manner more naturally regulated their diet.

Millions of Americans play on the theme of paranoia by living in fear of being *potential* victims of crime. It is true we have to take precautions to protect ourselves, but living in fear is not such a precaution. Some are so fearful they are ready to overhaul the Constitution to combat crime, advocating such measures as police sweeps of inner-city housing in search of guns and drugs.[1.]

A hidden psychological element appears to be creating more fear of crime than is warranted. We all carry irrational fears within ourselves that are projected outward into the environment. A person who expects to be seen by others in a negative light may be fearful to go to social events or to speak in public. A jealous person is fearful to introduce his girlfriend to others. A needy, insecure person is fearful of being alone. Often we believe inner fears such as these are validated by outer events and external circumstances. The more fearful we are, the more we see external circumstances such as the extent of crime as something that justifies our fear. If crime were non-existent or infrequent, we would experience fear in some other way, such as excessive worry about our children, our finances or jobs, national security, or through various phobias. Meanwhile, the gun-manufacturing industry, through its lobbies, persuades us that our fears are legitimate. It attempts to rationalize our fears in order to promote the sale of guns.

When we don't understand that such irrational fear is a creation of our emotional nature, we look into the environment to see where the fear is coming from, and thus create a paranoid perspective, the world view of the victim mentality. Law professor Robert Weisberg of Stanford University has written that "many Americans, projecting a variety of social insecurities onto the crime issue, seem captivated by the belief that they live in an era of unprecedented criminal epidemic..." He calls this a kind of historical egotism or arrogance—a sense that our time is unique, so different from "ordinary" times that fundamental changes in our constitutional principles must be made. "Many Americans," he adds, "now seem in love with the thought of being justified in their state of outrage."[2.]

Inner conflict induces us to create external enemies and fight them on the wrong battlefield. Was such paranoia an element in our fear of communism, and the communists' fear of us, during the Cold War? Did it contribute to the McCarthy period in the 1950's and the experience of the Vietnam War?

When we take responsibility for our fears, we are more likely to act against oppression in an effective way, rather than go on colluding in the feeling of being victims of it. Where the streets and neighborhoods have been taken back from drug dealers and other low-life, it has often been citizens, not the police, who made it happen. Coming together in a common purpose, these neighbors became responsible for overcoming their fears and halting the deterioration of their communities. Neither the police nor any other authority can make us as safe as we can make ourselves. Real safety abides on the other side of our paranoia and fear, where illusions have fallen away and we have come home to ourselves. Most of the time, as we discover, our fears are greatly overplayed and our helplessness is not so debilitating as first experienced.

The Social Impact of Feeling Insignificant

It is all or nothing: either we are somebody or we are nobody. Because we haven't yet realized our true essence, and have settled for an identity that is puny in comparison, we are frantic to justify our existence, defend our identity, enhance our self-image, and proclaim our worth. At times we are haunted by feelings of uselessness and experience the hurt of being nobody special. At this level of our evolvement, we are all capable of resonating emotionally with a conviction of our unworthiness, even as intellectually we believe in our value.

Being unworthy is not who or what we are. But like Charlie Brown it is what we are ready to believe about ourselves.

The feeling of being insignificant is quite apparent among our youth, particularly so among members of youth gangs. Gang members give each other a sense of respect and recognition that they are missing in their home lives and fail to muster on their own. They find respect from others for their strength, bravado, and violent powers. Weaker gang members take comfort in feeling accepted by powerful peers who take them into the fold. Being desperate for respect, and feeling blocked from socially acceptable achievements of it, they define respect in terms of risk and bravado, and so they risk violence and death in search of it. The resulting self-sabotage is of secondary concern to them, while the felt need to escape from a painful identity and establish a sense of power is primary.

A gang member is aware of how much he wants respect but inwardly he is contaminated by his attachment to disrespect. Masochistically, he is aligned with experiencing disapproval, neglect, and condemnation from others and from himself. This hinders him from conducting himself in a positive manner.

So what is a possible outcome when he is standing in a school yard with a gun hidden in his pants and some kid walks up and insults him? He pulls his gun and shoots the other boy. The "gunslinger" has acted aggressively, and it appears to us that his aggression is the problem. True, the act of aggression produced the killing. But where did the aggression come from? The killer obviously overreacted. His aggression is way out of proportion to the provocation. His aggression is an extreme defense designed to cover up the degree to which, on an inner level, the insulting words directed at him resonated with how he secretly feels about himself. He is masochistically attached to hearing degrading words from others, the kind of reproach and scorn he hears coming at him from his inner tyrant and likely from one or both of his parents. He may also have identified with a parent who is full of self-condemnation. This example shows the enormous self-defeat (going to jail) the boy is willing to accept in order to defend or protest against an awareness of his masochism, meaning in this case how he himself "takes a hit" on the feeling of being scorned, reduced, and negated.

He can't silence his inner tyrant (though suicide is often the result of an attempt to do just that) but he can shoot the boy who taunts him in the school yard. In doing so, he tries to prove (as a defense) that he hates being scorned and negated. His instinct at this point is to defend, however aggressively and self-destructively, against any awareness of his own readiness to absorb the insult and indulge in the feeling of it.

In the normal course of his day, the boy defends against inner accusations of his inadequacy by thinking or feeling, "I'm doing the best I can," or he may say to himself, "Life is too hard; my parents are too mean," or "Nobody understands me or supports me," or "It's true, I'm worthless and no good, and I don't give a damn."

Along comes a school-yard bully who mocks him just like his sarcastic parent or mocking inner voice. It is pay-off time. The gunslinger's immediate response is to cover up his attachment to feeling disrespected (and his willingness to "take a hit" on that feeling), by protesting through his unconscious defenses: "I'm not looking for that feeling of being "dissed." Look how angry I become when someone says I'm no good. I want respect and I'd better get it!"

Once he would have resorted to his fists to cover up his resonance with the insult. Now the stakes have been raised; a gun demands more respect. The gun is his defense against expected allusions to his unworthiness, and he is willing to shoot dead the person who says out loud what the gunslinger runs from, or tries to defend against, inside himself—his masochistic attachment to accusations of his unworthiness.

Because the boy's own sense of value is so diminished, the life of the other is of little significance and thus the consequence of pulling the trigger doesn't register until it is too late. In essence, he is killing himself.

The gunslinger's aggressive response illustrates the universal resistance to facing inner truth. When an insult is on target, meaning it corresponds directly with what the individual feels coming at him from his inner tyrant, the hurt and the sense of being offended is especially acute. Yet the need to cover up one's emotional resonance with the insult is even more acute. (Remember, the greatest secret in our inner world, and correspondingly in the outer world, is our emotional investment in self-hatred and self-aggression, which represents the masochism and the expression of it in our lives.)

This inner secret is so paradoxical, so challenging for us to assimilate, that it bears repeating: the young killer's macho posturing and false bravado (phony or pseudo-aggression) are marshaled in extreme degree to defend against his unconscious willingness to indulge in feeling devalued, put down, criticized, negated, and condemned. His violent act represents how ignorant (unknowing) he is of this attachment and how determined he is to remain ignorant of it. The gunslinger protests against the insult with extreme righteous indignation to cover up his emotional attachment to feeling discounted, criticized, and condemned. On the surface of his awareness he wants respect, but unconsciously he is drawn to and entangled in the feeling of the opposite.

In a cover story in *The Atlantic Monthly*, social scientist Elijah Anderson wrote that the rules of street code "provide a framework for negotiating respect. The person whose very appearance—including his clothing, demeanor, and way of moving—deters transgressions feels that he possesses...a measure of respect. With the right amount of respect, for instance, he can avoid 'being bothered' in public. If he is bothered, not only may he be in physical danger but he has been disgraced or 'dissed' (disrespected). Many of the forms that dissing can take might seem petty to middle-class people (maintaining eye contact for too long, for example), but to those invested in the street code, these actions become serious indications of the other person's intentions."[3.]

The more an individual is accused by his inner tyrant of being a loser, the more that evidence of his worth neutralizes the accusation and provides inner relief. Hence, money becomes disproportionately important as a means of establishing one's value. One commentator has written, "The worship of money is so intense that kids nickname themselves 'Money,' talk incessantly about 'loot,' and refer to stealing as 'getting paid.'"[4.]

A nineteen-year-old from Iowa, a member of a youth gang who murdered a seventeen-year-old girl, told police, "Money will get you power. Power and money are everything."[5.] His statement reflects the degree to which the youth felt himself to be without power, to be insignificant, and to have no value in his own right.

More Ways We Cover up Our Truth

All forms of antisocial or self-defeating behavior follow the same principles. Consider promiscuity, for example. On the surface, promiscuity is a sexual acting out, a desperate search for love. Underneath, however, it reflects an emotional conviction of being unloved. It is a symptom of one's self-hatred, self-abasement, and resistance to loving oneself. A promiscuous person resists feeling loved even when love is available to him or to her. Thus, this individual becomes engaged in a predictable, self-defeating acting out of his own self-abasement, covered up by a desperate attempt to prove that he wants love so badly he will take it any way he can.

We adopt a myriad of defenses to cover up our emotional attachments and our self-negating attitude toward ourselves, and these defenses can range from being mildly self-defeating, such as tardiness and procrastination, to being self-destructive, such as chronic anger or alcoholism. Other examples include compulsive gambling as a defense against an attachment to the feeling of losing; envy and greed as defenses against an attachment to feeling deprived and denied; a workaholic lifestyle to cover up the attachment to feeling inferior and unworthy; and loneliness as a symptom of the attachment to feeling abandoned and unwanted.

As another example, an individual who feels invisible without his spray-paint uses graffiti to draw attention to himself. His "artwork" makes him feel more visible, more substantial. Used as gang symbols to mark his territory, the graffiti identifies his turf and thus his presence and significance in the world. Though the graffiti constitutes negative exhibitionism in that it makes him look tawdry in the eyes of others, he feels respected by peers for his aggressiveness in spraying it in defiance of the law. Graffiti also makes this angry statement to the world: "Fine, so you think I'm insignificant and unworthy. Well, here's what I think of you and your precious property!" Graffiti also serves as a mode of attack, a pseudo-aggressive release against those one believes to be his victimizers.

Cigarette consumption among the young is influenced by advertising's promise of creating a "cool" impression. The implication that the individual is *not* "cool" without a cigarette resonates deep down with how the youth feels about himself. When his own sense of self is weak and plagued by self-doubt, and smoking enhances his image in the eyes of others, it is difficult for him to resist the temptation to smoke, or to care about himself enough to consider the consequences. In his inability to accept himself and feel good about himself, he is willing, even eager, to come under the influence of others for the trade-off in feelings of pseudo-acceptance. By also coming under the influence of the drug effect of cigarettes, he acts out his passivity in yet another way.

Someone who smokes twenty or more cigarettes a day frequently puts cigarettes in his mouth without taking responsibility for doing so. He doesn't make a conscious choice; he may realize after the fact that a fresh cigarette is stuck in his mouth. Thus, the problem of self-regulation is in part a lack of alertness and self-awareness. A smoker who decides to make a conscious choice for each cigarette he takes finds in this method more power of self-regulation. But the greater power comes from understanding that behind the apparent need for cigarettes are masochistic attachments to feelings of deprival, helplessness, disapproval, unworthiness, and being estranged from oneself. The real power of self-regulation comes from truly caring about oneself.

Feelings of being unworthy or insignificant also compel us to strive for fame, power, wealth, even notoriety. Achieving those goals allows us to claim, on an inner level: "Look how important I am. You see, I do have value, I am significant." Yet even were we to achieve our dreams of fame and wealth, we likely would continue to be haunted by feelings of self-doubt and unworthiness. Those feeling persist until we learn to accept and love ourselves without the need for external forms of validation.

Extremist and irrational positions abound when we are determined to defend ourselves against realization of our emotional attachments to feeling deprived, helpless, rejected, and abandoned. Some individuals claim to be extraterrestrial beings sent to earth to teach or reform us. These "aliens," unconsciously defending against feelings of being insignificant, act out their alienation from themselves by separating themselves from the human community. In feeling so unimportant, they exaggerate their importance beyond all rationality. They feel so powerless and incidental to themselves that they compensate by taking responsibility for the fate of the world. Yet in failing to see how their beliefs serve as a defense, they fail to take responsibility for themselves and to repair their alienation from themselves.

Cults tend to attract passive individuals who are easily influenced and directed by others. Cult members practice emotional dependence, the opposite of self-responsibility. They turn their power over to others and live according to the dictates and theories of leaders onto whom they have transferred the power and control they once bestowed on mother and father. This is the abdication of self-responsibility. Their compensation is to feel special as members of the cult, elevated and redeemed by their association with "higher truth" and powerful leaders. They may also set themselves up as superior to the rest of society and, in fortifying this defense against feelings of inferiority, feel compelled to rescue the rest of us from the error of our ways.

Racism is only superficially a factor of race or skin color. More significantly, it is an emotional problem produced by one's unconscious use of feelings of superiority and hatred as defenses against one's own conviction of inferiority and entanglement in self-hatred. The racist looks down on others because it makes him feel better about himself. The worse the racist feels about himself, the more he copes by projecting his self-hatred onto others. On the surface, he may be smug and superior. Typically, his self-image refuses even to consider that he is entangled in worthlessness and that he is secretly projecting his sense of worthlessness onto others. The only thing more painful to him than an interaction with an individual of another race or color is recognition of how deeply he believes in his own lack of value. Nonetheless, he is tortured by his inner tyrant which reminds him daily that he indeed feeds like a hungry bird on sensations of his own worthlessness. Minorities serve as external targets to redirect his self-aggression.

The racist is under a compulsion to make others experience what in his childhood he himself passively endured (feeling rejected, not valued, or condemned), or what he assimilated from his parents' emotional manner of interpreting life. He is compelled to make certain that other individuals or groups feel what he felt (and what he continues to feel toward himself)—unwanted and worthless. Because he has so little awareness of his emotional nature, he feels perfectly justified in his dislike or hatred of others, and uses as "evidence" for feeling this way any flaws or defects he can see in them.

Racists also have other emotional issues. They often feel the members of their target group are depriving or controlling them. They may feel deprived when a person of another skin color or nationality has a better job, or controlled when a minority member has authority over them. Their emotional interpretation of being victimized in this way by their foes convince racists even more firmly in the righteousness of their hatred.

In less extreme ways, we pay a huge price for our attachments to feeling deprived, controlled, criticized, and rejected. A person who is intellectually capable of becoming a professional or owning and operating a business never takes the plunge and goes on working for someone else for six dollars an hour because he doubts his abilities. Meanwhile, he is haunted daily by self-deprival, self-doubt, and self-criticism. Feelings of regret, guilt, and shame for not believing in himself may follow him to his grave.

Insecure people create misery all around. Some bureaucrats dream up unnecessary rules and regulations and add to the avalanche of paperwork because they feel the need to be important. Journalists dramatize situations out of proportion to the facts because it makes them feel more significant to initiate or to be part of a big story. Some parents, who in their low self-esteem are easily threatened and offended, react excessively and punish their children for being honest about their thoughts and feelings. Some doctors refuse to consider alternative medicines and therapies because they feel they will look bad in the eyes of their more traditional colleagues or that their studies and years of training will be invalidated. In all these examples, the individuals have masochistic attachments to the feeling of being seen as less than, unimportant, or in some other bad light, feelings that reflect the inadequacy they experience in themselves.

An example of an extreme case of this involves Colin Ferguson, the Long Island Railroad killer of 1994. Ferguson felt terribly angry and victimized.[6] He believed society's indifference and hostility to him merited his wrath. But Ferguson's wrath was really a consequence of, and a defense against, his own self-hatred and unconscious attachments to feeling neglected, rejected, and criticized.

Ferguson interpreted reality through an emotional veneer caused by his extreme negative view of himself, taking everything personally, being totally self-centered and in complete denial of his willingness to indulge in feeling victimized. Rather than see his own role or collusion in his misery and failure, and thus find a means of self-regulation, he blamed others for "making him" feel the way he did. The more he covered up his own suffering (caused by his passivity—the maintenance and reinforcement of his attachment to neglect, rejection, and disapproval), the angrier and more irrational he became. Thus, he would need to take extreme measures to "prove" to himself that those who opposed him were deserving targets of his violent impulses. He was steeped in self-hatred and condemned by his inner tyrant for allegedly being a failure, a nobody, and a loser. Ferguson placed responsibility for his failures and sense of victimization on innocents, acting out how he felt innocently abused and mistreated. As his inner conflict intensified, he fired away at the Long Island commuters with all the viciousness with which he attacked himself on an inner level. In a sense, he sacrificed the lives of others in a drama that mirrored his own wish to destroy himself.

To a less drastic degree, we all dump our "stuff" on others, or blame circumstances, or blame ourselves for the wrong reasons, rather than see and understand how we co-create the emotional dramas in our lives.

Self-sabotage may be running loose in our financial markets. As I write in the fall of 1998, no one knows for sure which way the volatile New York Stock Exchange and other such markets are headed. But it seems fair to say that, unless these high valuations represent a hidden form of inflation, individual stocks are overpriced, at least by traditional measures. We rush into overpriced markets because, in seeing others making easy money, we come under an inner accusation that we are losers or that we are missing out on the bonanza for not being in the game. We feel anxious sitting on the sidelines watching others reap easy pickings, feeling more deprived with every clang of the closing bell. The apparent crime is greed but the unconscious crime is the attachment to the feeling of losing out and missing the boat, reflecting our own inner criticism to being a loser and feeling that we are missing the boat in finding security and satisfaction in our lives.

Behind this market run-up of the last several years is also the fear, inflamed by Wall Street marketing during the past twenty years, that we will be helpless and abandoned in our old age without at least a few million dollars to retire on. The inner pressure builds until, no longer able to resist, we fling our savings into the market. When we understand the nature of this inner pressure, which reflects the insecurity we experience in ourselves, we are able to rise above the herd mentality and invest our funds with more awareness of these emotional factors.

As we peer into our financial future with the hidden intent of feeling loss and deprivation, we are convinced we are doing so out of genuine concern for our well-being. "I'm just trying to protect myself, to take care of myself, by seeing what the future brings," we say in our defense. But it is more insidious than that.

When we see how we use speculation about the future to feed our insecurities and alienation from ourselves, and undertake inner reform, we fall back on ourselves, on our relationship with ourselves, with others, and with existence, and thereby experience our true self in place of a void or fear.

Our entanglement in dissatisfaction and emptiness is a reason we are preoccupied with the notion of our salvation. In religious orthodoxy, salvation means redemption or freedom from our "sinful" selves. For thousands of years, we have been looking to be saved from responsibility for ourselves, from our fears, our powerlessness, our self-destructiveness, and our inability to love ourselves and others. We are bound to be anxious for salvation if we are abandoning, condemning, and rejecting ourselves. Instead of dreaming of salvation, we need to examine closely our feelings toward others and ourselves, as well as our past conditioning and how it impacts on us and our lives. As we break free of our limited identity, we discover our true self, a self we can accept, embrace, and love. This is our salvation.

In political terms, we see ourselves as free people. But we are not as free as we think when self-sabotage is on the rampage. As individuals, it is hard to find the best way forward when we can't tell where we are coming from. In order to grow, a person has to understand the relevant details of his or her history, just as a nation has to learn from its history by acknowledging and integrating its past mistakes and understanding the psychological dynamics behind present tensions and conflicts. Usually our impulse, personally and nationally, is to cover up the past and our mistakes. In doing so, we are more likely to repeat our mistakes, to flounder in predictable reaction rather than composed response, with pain and self-defeat the more likely consequences.

The following exercise can help you recognize your defenses and work through your entanglements with feelings of worthlessness.

1) Relate a recent or past experience in which you felt disapproved of, shamed, or bad about your performance. Describe in detail how you felt. Talk to your spouse or others about childhood experiences with regard to feeling shamed and disapproved of. See if you can recreate the feelings. The hurt that comes up is what you have remained attached to all these years. Isolate that hurt and sense that you are resistant to releasing it.

Feeling shame, embarrassment, bad, or worthless is the result of a claim-to-power defense (Example: "*I* cause people, through my faults, to look negatively upon me"). The defense, in this case, is employed to cover up the attachment from childhood to feeling criticized, looked down on, or seen as bad.

2) Write down your most common method of putting yourself down. Compare this with parental messages you received in childhood.

3) Describe some situations where you worry about how others see you. How do you imagine others see you? Compare with how you see yourself. Can you get a sense of how you are attached to the feeling of being seen in a negative light? Connect these feelings and expectations with how your parents saw you.

4) Answer the following: "If I allow myself to open up and express my genuine feelings, to express who I am, I expect others to…" Where in the past do these feelings come from? Were you able to be open and expressive with your parents? How would your parents respond if you were honest and open with them?

5) Make a list of the various ways that you judge and evaluate others. What are some of your common judgments of others? Is that how you judge and evaluate yourself? Being judgmental of others is a defense covering up your attachment to the feeling of being judged. Also, in being judgmental, you identify with the one being judged, thus indirectly immersing yourself in those feelings.

CHAPTER 9

Freedom From Self-Sabotage

When I drive up to Los Alamos I usually visit the Mesa Public Library, one of the best public libraries in the state. I like to sit in the lounge area soaking up the sweeping vista of the Jemez Mountains, the volcanic range a dozen miles west of the Rio Grande in north-central New Mexico. A few hundred yards away is the house in which Julius Robert Oppenheimer lived in the 1940's when he and his team of scientists built the two atomic bombs dropped on Japan.

It is not surprising that in this century the atom may have been more accessible to human understanding than the psyche. Discoveries such as atomic power excite our egotism while knowledge of the psyche threatens it. I remember seeing in a magazine a 1950's photograph that showed three men posing in front of the controls of a just-activated nuclear reactor. One of three gazed upon the controls with a radiantly triumphant expression, his face in a luminous glow, his eyes lit up with kilowatts of pride. How intoxicating it is to create and control such power! It is a hallmark of self-sabotage that we get excited about something that has the potential to destroy us and are indifferent or even hostile to what is in our best interest.

We know a lot about nuclear reactions but not as much about human reactions. But it is human reactions in ourselves, in the family, the community, the nation, and the world that are demoralizing, sabotaging, and killing us.

Some individuals are willing to use our latest technology to produce human clones. Is it really wise to reproduce ourselves without understanding our unconscious malevolence? We may soon have the technology to create a pseudo-immortality when computers scan our thoughts, memories, emotions, load them into silicone chips and insert them into the "brains" of total body prostheses. If we don't have human nature figured out by then, we might end up playing ourselves in the "reality version" of a Hollywood action movie, having to vanquish the human clones that became our deadly enemies.

Carl Jung wrote a short book published in 1957 and titled *The Undiscovered Self* in which he pleaded for humankind to appreciate the vital importance of understanding the unconscious mind. The alternative to self-destructiveness, Jung wrote, requires not mass movements for good or idealistic pleas for reason but a true understanding of the inner self which recognizes the existence of good and evil within ourselves. In his view, the unconscious has been ignored "out of downright resistance to the mere possibility of there being a second psychic authority besides the ego. It seems a positive menace to the ego that its monarchy can be doubted."[1] A lack of insight deprives us of the capacity to deal with evil, he wrote. Underestimation of the psychological factor, he added, "is likely to take a bitter revenge."[2]

Honest examination of the unconscious is humbling because it shatters our self-image, our tenuous definition of ourselves, and shakes up our self-centeredness and self-negation. The experience is challenging and can be quite intense, but as we break through and scamper past the debris of our delusions, we emerge on the other side with something in our possession of incalculable value. We know from thousands of ancient myths and stories that the hero in the making is required to plunge into a dark underworld filled with menacing, archetypal villains and creatures who resist his progress and oppose his very being. He emerges from the dark underworld strengthened and enlightened, sufficiently purified to be worthy of the grace of God—a Golden Fleece or a Holy Grail that signifies reunion with his true self.

Our best books and movies are infused with the high drama that pits good against evil, whether ancient battles between St. Michael and Lucifer or futuristic ones between Luke Skywalker and Darth Vader. We relate so strongly to these heroic myths and stories because they represent our own inner struggles between the part of us that wants to be victorious in life—ultimately, to merge with our true self and realize the divine within—and the inner tyrant that opposes this destiny.

The unconscious is understood to be the gateway to spiritual experience. Though some prefer to believe the unconscious is nothing more than primal chaos or the information base of an animal nature, it is in my opinion an inner space as glorious in its microcosmic creation as outer space is in the macrocosmic (and perhaps these spaces merge in unitary wholeness). It is through the unconscious, through the unfolding of our own being, that we discover our eternal spirit and its oneness with divine essence.

Of course, this contention that we can know God through our own being raises objections from traditionalists among Christians, Jews, and Muslims who believe fervently that the deciding factor in religious life is our allegiance to historical revelation coming down from on high. That we can commune directly with God and find Him in our hearts were central beliefs of the Gnostic movement, one of the most long-lived branches of early Christianity. After centuries of struggle, however, the Gnostic Scriptures were declared heretical and the movement was eradicated by the established church.

We have many different creeds and religions claiming to represent absolute truth. Their concepts of absolute truth, however, have not brought us closer to loving ourselves, humanity, and all life forms with sufficient acceptance and compassion. Nor can we find absolute truth through science. In 1927, physicists put forward the Copenhagen Interpretation of Quantum Mechanics which discarded the previous assumption of science that absolute truth can be found in nature. What the scientists proclaimed has now become the paradigm, that we cannot assume an objective reality apart from our experience. At the subatomic basis of matter, all we can know are probabilities, meaning how, as we observe them, particles and streams of light and energy are likely to behave or to function. The new physics is based not on absolute truth but on how we correlate and accommodate what we observe with what we experience.

So who is to be our authority on the truth—the one with the most borrowed knowledge or you and I? Who knows better than us, we who have endeavored through our own experience to determine the truth of our existence? Let us put our belief in the golden nuggets of revelation we have refined from the excavation of our own inner depths.

This knowing is formless. It can't be put in the palm of your hand. It can't be put into words, nor presented as a field of knowledge. All we can do is follow the steps and the direction provided by our own inner guidance.

As we approach this level of knowing ourselves, we are creating a strong foundation for asserting, accepting, and loving ourselves, and for making the wisest choices for our well-being. When we are moving toward this truth, we cannot be persuaded to believe any nonsense or to follow any fool, especially the sabotaging fool within us.

Exploring our selves and finding our truth is an adventure. You might feel like an explorer descending into a secret cavern, a diver plunging to the bottom of a hidden pool, a tracker pursuing a beast into its lair, a glider flinging himself off a cliff. Courage is the attribute that launches our adventure and keeps us moving forward.

You take the plunge through your willingness to look at yourself. Your wish is to see and know the truth about yourself. For instance, if you are plagued by feelings of anger, resist the temptation to splatter it on others or to feel that it is validated by a difficult situation in your life. Follow it to its source inside of you. Reactive anger is often a defense to cover up your willingness to take on feelings such as being refused, controlled, and rejected.

Be present to yourself and observe yourself as you enter into your feelings. You won't lose yourself. A part of you knows the way back. If shame comes up, just observe it. The shame is not you. If fear comes up, observe it. Be curious about it, find out what it means. The fear is not you. You won't be annihilated by it. Nor will you be torn asunder by anger, disgust, sadness, loneliness, hopelessness, worthlessness, or a wish to die. Just observe whatever comes up. These are not you. Be curious about what you experience and look behind the experience for the source of the feelings. Where do they come from in your past? How do they reflect how you feel about yourself?

The need to recognize and to understand unconscious self-hatred is crucial in a program to eliminate self-sabotage. But there is another step in the process. Neutralizing the influence of our dark side also leads us into an experience of the essence of ourselves—our soul, our true self. Edmund Bergler's great discoveries were presented in scientific terms, in mental and emotional language. The extension of this knowledge into the spiritual realm can lead to greater resolution of self-sabotage and higher levels of wholeness and self-fulfillment. I believe that true psychological emancipation is not possible without restoration of our connection to our true self.

Most people do not recognize that we have a true self within us. They may believe intellectually that we have a soul or spirit, but what they really feel (and what they identify with) is their personality, a false self, and the self-image that protects it. This false self is our misunderstanding of who and what we are.

As previously mentioned, many of us spend our time running from ourselves or distracting ourselves—with projects, daydreaming, mental speculations, substance abuse, various forms of stimulation, material possessions, and a thousand trivial pursuits. We also place an undue emphasis on the value of external accomplishments, acquisitions, and goals because we are not feeling the value inherent in ourselves.

We cling to our false self and our self-image for fear of discovering the truth about ourselves, namely our self-hatred, our masochistic tendencies, our cherished stash of hurts and grievances, and, yes, our resistance to acknowledging our divine heritage.

Whatever disharmony or conflict we experience with others or with situations in our daily lives reflects on our relationship with our true self. In fact, everything we experience is a reflection of our relationship with our true self. Whatever irritates us about our spouse, children, friends, or parents is what irritates us about ourselves—and it is also what separates us from our self.

How much time do we spend listening to ourselves and understanding our own feelings? Do we know at a given moment what we are feeling? Or is the feeling just there, with no consciousness on our part that is alert and sensitive to it? Do we know what we appreciate about ourselves, or do we focus on our negative aspects? What is it about us we want to keep hidden?

Connection with our true self happens on a feeling level. It is at this level, rather than on a mental level, that we can best cultivate the self-awareness that leads us to our truth. Individuals often become quite emotional when, as an exercise or technique, they begin to dialogue with their self. In this technique, a person engages in a dialogue between his self and his personality. The dialogue can be initiated with one of the following questions posed by the self.

How are you feeling right now? How do you feel about me? Why don't you want to know me? Why are you afraid of me? Why do you push me away? Why do you squash me?

The questions can be even more personal and effective when we address ourselves by name: Sally, how come you don't like me? Bill, why do you hate me? Jack, why don't you believe in me? Why don't you trust me, Deborah? Why don't you want me, Jean? Why don't you value me, George?

Other questions include: Why won't you help me? Why do you feel undeserving? How do you see me? Why are you afraid to get close to me? Why don't you take care of me? Why don't you love me?

A person might have his self say to him at a difficult moment in his day, "How are you feeling, (person's name)? It's a tough situation right now, isn't it? I think you're handling it very well. Do you know why you lost your patience a moment ago? You're doing the best you can and I support you fully." This communication certainly contrasts with our inner tyrant's penchant to be mocking, demeaning, and vicious toward ourselves.

A dialogue might also proceed in this way:

True Self: Why don't you love me?

Personality: Because you're worthless. I'm disgusted by you.

True Self: Why?

Personality: Because you're inadequate. You can't do anything right. You fail at everything you try to do.

True Self: Where do those feelings come from?

Personality: Well, that's how I felt my parents regarded me. I've been over this a hundred times. I'm sick of it all!

True Self: Please tell me again what happened.

Personality: Well, they discouraged me from going to college, telling me it would be a waste of time. They were never really interested in my academic studies. Every time I did something, my father found fault with it, telling me, "Can't you do anything right? What's your problem?"

True Self: As you know, this means that you are doing to yourself what your parents did to you. How does it feel to put yourself down like that?

Personality: I feel valueless, worthless, that my life doesn't make a difference. I'm unwanted and unloved.

True Self: I know it feels that way. But you *are* loved. I love you. Try to believe in yourself. You and I are one. I am always here for you.

The feelings can deepen as we continue to dialogue. The deeper we can feel ourselves, and be honest with what we are feeling, the more we can extricate ourselves from our self-hatred and self-negation.

As you dialogue, try to feel whatever comes up, whether sadness, despair, hopelessness, longing, compassion, or love. Can you feel compassion for that part of yourself that is crying out for recognition and union? Can you see how you, yourself, refuse to nurture and support yourself?

Cultivating a relationship with one's true self is like planting a seed and providing it the water and nutrients it needs to grow. It takes time before the plant breaks ground and we can see that our labors are bearing fruit. Initially, in dialoguing with the self or in trying to feel the self, we may experience that not much is happening. The process takes time. Continue the dialoguing. Tell yourself how important it is for you to begin to make this contact. *Feel* how much you want this contact to happen.

You can understand this process of establishing a new relationship with yourself by imagining you are the wise, loving mother or father that you wanted and yearned for as a young child. You regard your child with love and speak to him with sensitivity and respect. You love him regardless of how smart or handsome or adept he is. You cherish his very being as he is. Can you begin to feel how you could establish a similar relationship with yourself?

Most of us feel that our parents were not sufficiently sensitive to us and did not fully appreciate our unique being. Often they saw us simply as extensions of themselves. Consequently, we are not sensitive to and appreciative of our true self. Now we can be that wise parent to our own unique being. We can transform the impoverished relationship within ourselves by speaking and relating to ourselves in a nurturing and supporting manner.

As we enter this process, we begin to experience more sensitivity for ourselves, and we are particularly compassionate to ourselves for the pain and hurt we have experienced. Increasingly, we understand that our misconceptions, inappropriateness, and passivity were predictable outcomes based on our limited understanding at that time. In other words, it wasn't our fault. Self-forgiveness develops as we understand that our past reactions were the only option we had, based on our conditioning and awareness. Similarly, forgiveness of others results when we understand how their conditioning, self-centeredness, and masochism have them locked in a limited behavioral and emotional range. As we embrace ourselves in this new way, we integrate fully the rejected parts of ourselves and love ourselves.

In this quest to find our real value as human beings and to feel ultimately fulfilled, we can't count on much help from a culture which emphasizes materialism, money, power, image, and celebrity. We have to come home to ourselves and realize what we have lost. We do so by becoming explorers on the frontier of who we truly are, searching for the great magic and mystery of our being.

Many of us will take the challenge to face our deeper aspects if we have a road map and if we believe our effort will be rewarded. We are ready to seize knowledge that will free us of negative emotions and self-defeating behaviors. Behind our determination is the increased inner pressure for us to account for our continuing unhappiness in an age of material abundance and leisure time. We have unlocked the secret of the atom, so we can and will do the same about human nature. We are ready to explode the weaker theories about human nature that have taken root in our universities, treatment centers, and social-policy discourses and that have left us stranded in dead-end impasses.

We are caught between an old and a new way of thinking and understanding. The old way isn't working anymore. Yet, emotionally, it feels so threatening to give it up. We are used to the old way, the old identity. Even though it is painful and no longer works, we can't quite cast it aside. We hesitate, not knowing what will replace it.

The old way, represented by our unrestrained self-aggression, is associated by us with survival and self-preservation. We don't know who we are without it. Paradoxically, we feel we will perish without our old identity, but in fact it imperils us.

Each of us is born into the world to grow and learn, beginning when pressure builds up in the womb to dislodge us from our primal consciousness. We are thrust into the birth canal to enter a strange new dimension that forces discovery and responsibility upon us.

Nature is dynamic, not static. It is about death and rebirth, regression and progression. Every summer dies into winter and is reborn in spring, bringing death to the old, birth of the new, in a process that has ensured our continuity. Surely we will move forward now to make new discoveries about our nature, and to embrace and refine our being as we overcome self-sabotage.

Solutions and Exercises

Taking Responsibility for an Emotional Issue

1) First describe the situation that is contributing to your emotional distress. Give the details of what is happening (or has happened) and how you are reacting (or reacted). What is the other person (or situation) doing to you? For example, "He lectured me for an hour about how inadequate I am."

2) Now describe the feelings you experienced. Were you angry, depressed, sad, or fearful? For example, "I felt rejected, unimportant, and criticized." Or "I felt gypped and deprived of what I want."

3) Go back into your childhood and recall an incident or incidents that bring up the same feelings. For example, who lectured you in your past? How did that feel?

4) Run through your life and recall how you have experienced those same feelings in different contexts and with different individuals. Note the predominance of those feelings, for instance rejection, criticism, deprival, and so on, throughout your life.

5) Give examples of how you may have provoked the same reactions in others. For example, do you lecture others and criticize them in the same way that you were just lectured? The traits you despise in others are usually your own. If you feel that the other is withholding love, ask yourself, "How do I withhold

love as well?"

6) Describe how you subject yourself to the same treatment you feel others subject you to. For example, how often do you lecture and relentlessly criticize yourself?

The Agony of Guilt

Guilt, the feeling that one deserves to be punished, is one of the most common ways we negate ourselves. Most often feelings of guilt are completely inappropriate to a situation. Of course, guilt is appropriate if you beat your wife or rob a bank. But most of the time we feel guilty for minor or even nonexistent infractions. Guilt feelings disappear when we understand and work though the underlying feelings.

The following exercise can help you identify how you use guilt as a defense to cover up your investment in self-denial and self-rejection.

1) List all the behaviors or actions you still feel guilty about.

2) Give examples of when other people have "laid" guilt trips on you and how you responded.

3) Give examples of the guilt trips you lay on yourself.

4) Give examples of guilt trips you have laid on others.

5) Give examples of guilt trips that your parents laid on you while you were growing up and later as an adult. Did you ever lay guilt trips on them, such as trying to make them feel responsible for your feelings or life situations?

6) Try to become aware of what negative emotion hides behind your guilt. For instance, is your guilt a reaction to your indulgence in feeling rejected or criticized?

Parental Patterns

Many of us have a hard time remembering how we felt in

our interactions with our parents. These feelings may be consciously forgotten but they remain in the unconscious awaiting opportunities to surface. As mentioned, we transfer hurtful feelings experienced with our parents and siblings onto circumstances or people in the present.

It is liberating to understand how you interpreted your parents' behavior toward you and how you modeled yourself on their strengths and weaknesses. By reconnecting with these old hurts and grievances, we become conscious of how we anticipate and promote these feelings in the present. The purpose here isn't to blame our problems on our parents, of course, but to see and understand how we still play out being victims of their real or alleged malice or neglect.

Some of these questions are similar to those in the work-history profile at the end of Chapter 6. However, they are important and relevant questions in this new context. Reflect on and answer the following:

1) Did your parents allow you to express your feelings openly or were you afraid to reveal what you thought or felt? Were you ever punished or made to feel bad for expressing these feelings?

Are you afraid now to express and reveal your feelings in your personal relationships? What do you expect will happen if you do?

2) Describe the communication pattern in your family. Were verbal exchanges sarcastic, judgmental, superficial, nonexistent, and so on? Describe the quality of communication in your past or present relationships.

3) When you had a problem as a child, did your parents make it your fault, tease you, ridicule you, disapprove of you, protect you, ignore you, pamper you, make excuses for you, dismiss you, or discount you? Do you still experience these same feelings in your life? How and when?

4) Did your parents support your growing independence? Did they ask you questions about how you felt or perceived events? Did they allow you to participate in and make your own decisions? Or did you have to conform to their way of thinking and behaving?

To what degree do you believe that you act independently and autonomously today?

5) Did your parents treat you with respect? Did they see you as a unique individual with needs and dreams? Did they recognize your talents? Or were you used to satisfy their needs? Were you invisible to them?

How have these feelings affected your feelings about yourself today and your ability to be expressive?

6) Did you ever feeling unwanted by them? Were you a source of delight to them? Or were you supposed to make them look good?

Do you have similar feelings with your friends and relationships?

7) What measures did your parents use to control your behavior? Such measures might include threats, guilt, shame, intimidation, bribery, and sugary praise.

Explore these same control measures in your present relationships.

8) Were your parents able to admit their mistakes and take responsibility for their behaviors? Or did they deny any wrongdoing and blame others for their faults?

Are you involved with someone with the same problem? Explore the degree to which you accept criticism and admit your mistakes.

9) Consider the extent to which you were praised and criticized by your parents. Did they put pressure on you to perform?

How has their response to you affected your ability to perform today? Are you still reacting to their negative judgments?

10) Did interactions with your parents produce fear or guilt or feelings of well-being?

Do you feel fear or guilt in your interactions with others?

Fueling the Emotional Imagination

The visual drive or emotional imagination can become our worst enemy. The emotional imagination is always ready to create thoughts, feelings, beliefs, and scenarios that resurrect old emotional memories which in turn lead us into self-defeating behaviors.

Where do negative scenarios come from? They are produced by our emotional attachments to the primary feelings listed in Chapter 2. The following exercise helps readers to understand how these primary feelings represent unresolved issues from childhood that plague us still and fuel the emotional imagination.

(1) Write down the most prominent negative scenarios you have recently experienced, been tempted to visualize, or conceivably been obsessed by. Examples include being killed in a car accident, starving in the gutter, being rejected by a lover or spouse, or being exposed as a fake and a fraud. To come up with these scenarios, it might help if you ask, "What have I been afraid of lately?"

(2) Now look into the memories of your childhood. Ask yourself, "Are any of the *feelings* (not the scenario itself) similar to feelings I had in my childhood?" For example, a fear of flying and, of course, crashing usually goes back to childhood. The fear may be a consequence of how, as a child, you didn't trust your parents. You might have felt they were going to let you down and not take care of you in some way. Now you have

transferred that fear (the expectation of being let down) onto the pilot of any airplane you fly in.

(3) For each worst-case scenario you come up with, look for your bottom-line attachment, meaning your unconscious willingness to indulge in some old negative issue and feeling. Now you can begin to take responsibility for that negative feeling by seeing how you secretly maintain and reinforce it.

Finding the Middle

Step 1: List all the behaviors and patterns that you feel you are having difficulty regulating. For example, overeating, drinking too much coffee, inability to cut back on work hours, overspending, and so on. For each one, let an image come that reflects that part of you that seems determined to continue with this behavior.

a. Have this part of you answer the following question: "I don't want to stop doing this because.... " Next, list all the feelings and reasons this part gives for resisting balance, for instance, "It's too boring," or "I like the taste," or "I just want to do what I want to do."

b. Scan your memory and see if you can determine where these feelings or behavior originated. Were either of your parents involved with the same unbalanced behavior, perhaps in its opposite version. For example, if you are a workaholic, maybe your father was lazy and irresponsible. Do this for each behavior. And spend some time exploring these patterns in your past.

c. Now let an image come of another part of you that is critical and scornful of this first part's behavior. For example, "Why are you doing this to yourself? You're disgusting. You have no will; you're a mushball." Write out all the ways you reproach yourself for your feelings and behaviors.

d. Does this reproachful voice sound like your mother or

your father? Is it one of your siblings? This voice represents your inner tyrant and it reflects the words or thoughts of your parents or siblings and what you imagined they thought or felt about you.

e. Take a step back and observe the struggle that has been going on in you for some time now. Can you see how fruitless the struggle is? Realize that this struggle is all you know and that it would be scary to let it go.

Step 2: Imagine now a third part of you that is beyond both the weak part and the critical part. This new part represents your true self. Have this part address both the weak part and the critical part, and become a mediator between the two. Write down this true self's suggestions for resolving this problem. Trust yourself. You do know what is best for you. Let your essence come forward. Instinctively, we have what it takes to balance our behaviors and resolve our emotions.

The Observer in You

When you learn to observe, without judgment, your thoughts, fantasies, and emotional reactions, you have taken a big step in regulating them. Take some time out each day to chart the following:

1) Your thoughts or feelings about others. This includes becoming aware of feeling their pain; trying to solve their problems; how you might confront them; what they think about you or how they might react to you; what they have done to you or how they hurt you (past or recent past) or are going to hurt you; analyzing their weaknesses or flaws; considering how they disappointed you; seeing critical judgments you make about them; and noticing any positive or negative fantasies about someone.

2) Your thoughts and feelings about yourself. Do you engage in put-downs, reproaches, and other forms of self-criticism? Do

you focus on past failures or blunders? Are you tempted to experience negative expectations about yourself and your life, saying or feeling, for instance, "I'll never amount to anything."

3) Whether you replay past grievances or emotional injuries? Examples include the memory and feeling of not being invited to a party, a friend not calling you back, major or minor betrayals experienced with friends, children, parents, or siblings.

4) Your daydreams. Are you concerned with what is going to happen in the future? This includes thoughts about impending catastrophes. What are your fears about the future?

5) Whether you focus on lists and chores to be done. Do you have a drill-sergeant in your head? Are you preoccupied with not getting things done?

6) How much time you spend reflecting on a) deprivation— not getting what you want or (as a defense against that feeling) daydreaming of riches and privilege; b) control issues—feeling dominated, pushed around, or (as a defense against that feeling) dreaming of being completely free and having no responsibilities; c) rejection—not being recognized or seen as important or (as a defense against that feeling) being loved and admired by all.

Make It a Hobby, Not a Chore

One man told me, "It just seems so hard, doing what's required to grow and develop. It's all a big maze. I don't know if I can do this."

"Do it like a hobby," I said. "Some people find it fun, for instance, to set up a workshop in their garage and tinker there with their hobby in the evenings and on the weekends. Instead of a garage, imagine that you set up an inner workshop. You take it with you everywhere. And you tinker there with new knowledge, memories, feelings, observations, and exercises. In this workshop, you don't set goals, undertake projects, or lift heavy weights. Instead, you let the material float around in space, and you watch to see what comes together, what fits in place. You just play with what you have and what you're learning. It all comes together as your new knowledge is processed through daily experiences. Experiment with your insights and ideas. Go light and easy."

The following exercises, adapted from Roberto Assagiolli's book, *The Act of Will*, are perfect for tinkering in your traveling workshop.

Exercise 1

Go through a day saying to yourself, for every action you undertake, "I am choosing to do this; this is my choice."

Make it a choice to do what you are doing, even for ordinary, everyday things. Say, for instance, "I'm choosing to do laundry today. This is what I choose to do. I am making this choice."

This is different from, "I have to do laundry today." Watch how many choices you make. Do you slip into using *have to?* Do you ask others what to do? If so, ask yourself if you are not secretly willing to go about your activities feeling forced and controlled.

Once you have done this for a day, look at your whole life in terms of the decisions you have made, choices you have made, and what has been motivating those choices.

Now examine whether or not you apply the power of will to the choices you make. How much resistance do you experience? What sort of feelings come up when you find that your will is flagging and you are unable to continue on a chosen course? Do you feel forced, controlled, or deprived? Maybe your will is weak because you have a secret agenda to be disappointed in yourself, and then to criticize or disapprove of yourself, or to imagine that a parent, boss, or spouse is disappointed in you.

Remember, your own hidden emotional attachments are what you are most reluctant to see.

Exercise 2

Do something you have never done before.

Make a plan and follow it.

Get up and do whatever you have been delaying.

Postpone an action you would prefer to do immediately.

Act without hesitation on a minor choice.

Do something worthwhile that makes you feel insecure.

Refrain from saying something you are tempted to say.

Exercise 3

What do you believe you *can't* do that you would like to do? Select a reasonable goal you always believed you couldn't attain. Write out the steps that would be required to achieve that goal.

For example, suppose you wanted to be a public speaker, or at least able to speak competently in public, but feel that your fears prevent you. Steps would include learning more about your fears. Are you attached to being seen in a negative light? Where does that come from? Was your mother or father fearful in this way? Get books on public speaking. Enroll in speech classes. Ask friends to listen to your talks on different subjects. Make it happen.

A Guide to Self-Responsibility

To be effective, these maxims and attitudes have to be understood emotionally, not just intellectually. That means we need to understand how and why it is so hard for us to follow this guide.

1) Life is unfair and provides a steady diet of annoyances and

obstacles. We won't always be successful, even when we try our best. It is your job to neutralize problems internally and regard them as challenges to develop more personal strength.

2) Accept the fact there will be disappointments in your life. We all have problems and let-downs. Learn to accept them with grace. Ideally, we are able to accept even the hardships of life with grace and dignity.

3) Watch out for the secret willingness to indulge in disappointment. Don't be surprised by an unfavorable turn of events or feel that life is against you. A sure way to cultivate disappointment is to expect too much. Don't expect others to cater to you and instantaneously provide for your needs. Life isn't intended to conform to your expectations or wishes. Accept the weaknesses of others without feeling let down.

4) Cultivate a sense of proportion. A self-responsible person makes the distinction between a pin-prick and a dangerous wound. Keep in mind that you are not always deliberately victimized by someone else's disagreeable action. Watch the tendency to maximize the potential worry or suffering of minor annoyances.

5) Don't personalize fate. The seemingly aggressive actions of those around you aren't necessarily meant to attack you personally. Recognize that other people have their own perceptions and their own problems. Be curious and open to their feelings and beliefs. Accept differences in others without taking it personally.

6) Believe in yourself and your convictions, even if they go against the grain. A self-responsible person doesn't need others to agree with him or to validate his opinions. We don't have to be right or perfect all the time. We have to be comfortable with limitations we can't change. You want to be able to admit when you are wrong or when you don't know the answer.

7) Don't do for others what they can do for themselves. A healthy person doesn't feel compelled to rescue or save others, but realizes that they have to work hard and sometimes struggle in order to develop their will and a strong sense of self.

8) Begin to distinguish when and how the problems in your life are self-created and self-maintained.

9) No one is to blame for your emotional disturbances. All your emotional reactions originate in you, although they may seem to be triggered by others. It is primarily our perceptions and interpretations of events that cause our suffering.

Concrete Steps to Self-Fulfillment

1) *Regulation of your health and well-being.* How well do you eat? Make room in your life for exercise, play, hobbies, and nature. Are you able to regulate your eating and drinking habits? Do you rely on drugs of any kind to get by?

2) *Regulation of your emotional health.* Learn to take responsibility for your emotional reactions, behaviors, or negative attitudes. Don't blame your feelings and behaviors on others, or depend on others to make you feel good about yourself.

Do you expect that others will rescue you or take care of you? Are you able and willing to earn your own living rather than depend on hand-outs? Do you make excuses or rationalizations for your dependency?

3) *Helping your children learn regulation.* Become concerned with your children's emotional well-being and happiness. Participate in their lives and allow them to express who they are. Don't try in a rigid, controlling manner to make them conform to your values and lifestyle. Make sure they are taught to respect the feelings of others and to value all life by being an example of that compassionate respect.

Do you allow them at appropriate times to make their own

decisions and to express their own opinions, even if they are different from yours? Do you do for them what they can do for themselves? Do you try to rescue them and make their lives completely free of pain or struggle? Disappointments are inevitable. Allow them to feel.

4) *Caring for the environment and future generations.* Take concrete responsibility for preserving the environment, whether in your own house, yard, community, or planet. Look into how you can make your house and activities more pollution-proof. Take the same attitude about the environment you would to a campground. You are using that space for a temporary period. Leave that space as you found it, or clean or beautify it, so that others will have the benefit of using it. Treat your animals and all animals with respect, just as you yourself would want to be treated. Ask yourself, how will our actions affect our great-grandchildren?

5) *Responsible employers.* Treat your employees as human beings, not as automatons to be squeezed dry for your own benefit. Treat them as you would want to be treated. Validate their contributions and have concern for their feelings. You don't have to rescue them, take care of their personal lives, or feel responsible for their happiness. But give constructive, compassionate help rather than criticism. You set the tone. Give each person a chance to feel important.

6) *Responsibility of employees.* Don't expect your employer to act as a parent who dispenses approval or disapproval, or is somehow supposed to rescue you or take care of your personal life. Do your job with pride and integrity—the best you can do. Elevate your job, no matter how menial, by bringing your good intentions and dignity to it. Be open to others and see them as fellow travelers on similar adventures. We all need each other as part of one great consciousness.

7) *Responsibility of government representatives.* Become

impeccable and move beyond your own self-interest into a larger concern for the common good. Stick to your word; do what you say. Your word should be considered sacred, not a tool for winning votes and popularity. Representatives need to incorporate all the above points in their attitudes and behaviors.

8) *Responsible citizens.* Don't tolerate corruption and don't indulge in feeling victimized by it. Support the most genuine candidates for office, those who you determine are not motivated by self-aggrandizement or naive ideologies. Require them to stick to their word. Give up the notion that the government is a source of entitlement. The government doesn't exist to rescue you or to make others comply with your views. Give up the attitude that "the government will take care of it." That's a carry-over from our parental expectations of childhood. If we act as children, we will be treated and regulated as children. Form community support groups to take charge of local concerns rather than wait for others do it.

Notes

Chapter 2

1. Erich Fromm. *The Heart of Man: Its Genius for Good and Evil.* Harper and Row, New York, 1964. p. 120.

Chapter 3

1. Erich Fromm. *The Heart of Man.* p. 73.
2. Abraham Maslow. *Toward a Psychology of Being.* Van Nostrand Reinhold Co. New York, 1968. p. 200.
3. Benjamin Franklin. *The Autobiography.* Quoted in *The American Tradition in Literature.* Gosset and Dunlap. 1974. p. 139.
4. Jean Piaget. *The Moral Judgment of the Child.* The Free Press. New York, 1965. p. 394.
5. Erik H. Erikson. *Insight and Responsibility.* W.W. Norton & Co. New York, 1964. p. 44.
6. *Ibid.* p. 44.
7. *Ibid.* p. 45.
8. "Erik Erikson, 91, Psychoanalyst Who Reshaped Views of Human Growth, Dies." As quoted in *The New York Times.* May 13, 1994.
9. Will Henry. "A Time to Talk of Heroes." As quoted by Dale L. Walker in his Introduction to *Journey to Shiloh.* Bantam Books, New York, 1990.
10. Alexander Lowen, M.D. *Narcissism: Denial of the True Self.* Macmillan Publishing. New York, 1983. p. ix.
11. Barbara W. Tuchman. *The March of Folly: From Troy to Vietnam.* Ballantine Books. New York, 1984.

Chapter 4

1. Gary Zukav. *The Dancing Wu Li Masters. An Overview of the New Physics.* Bantam edition. New York, 1980. p. 27.

Chapter 6

1. Peter Gay, Ed. *The Freud Reader.* W.W. Norton & Co. New York, 1989. p. 558.
2. *Ibid.* p. 760.
3. Edmund Bergler. *The Superego.* International Universities Press. Madison, CT. (1989 printing.) copyright 1952. As quoted in the Forward, p. xviii.

Chapter 7

1. Edmund Bergler, *Divorce Won't Help.* Liveright Publishing Corp., New York. Reprint with New Introduction 1960. p. 240.
2. Edmund Bergler, *The Revolt of the Middle-Aged Man.* International Universities Press. New York. 1954, 1957, 1985. pp. 80-81.
3. Edmund Bergler, *Principles of Self-Damage.* Philosophical Library. New York, 1959. p. 449.
4. Peter Gay, Ed. *The Freud Reader.* W.W. Norton & Co,. New York, 1989. p. 754.
5. *Ibid.* p. 622.
6. Edmund Bergler, *The Writer and Psychoanalysis.* International Universities Press. Madison, CT. 1986. p.14.

Chapter 8

1. Robert Weisberg. "Are criminals forcing us to overhaul the constitution?" *The New Mexican,* May 1, 1994.
2. *Ibid.*
3. Elijah Anderson. "The Code of The Streets." *The Atlantic Monthly.* May, 1994. p. 82.

4. Greg Donaldson. "Throwaway Youth." *The New York Times.* July 3, 1994.

5. Don Terry. "Killed by Her Friends, Sons of the Heartland." *The New York Times.* May 18, 1994.

6. "Black Rage: In Defense of a Mass Murderer." *Time,* June 6. 1994. p. 31.

Chapter 9

1. C.G. Jung. *The Undiscovered Self.* New American Library. New York, 1958. p. 98.

2. *Ibid.* p. 105.

Bibliography

Assagioli, Roberto. *The Act of Will.* Penguin Books, Baltimore, 1974.

Bergler, Edmund. *Curable and Incurable Neurotics.* Liveright, NY. 1961, 1972.

Bergler, Edmund. *Money and Emotional Problems.* Doubleday, New York, 1951.

Bergler, Edmund. *Principles of Self-Damage.* Philosophical Library, New York, 1959.

Bergler, Edmund. *Selected Papers of Edmund Bergler, MD. 1933-1961.* Grune & Stratton, New York, 1969.

Bergler, Edmund. *The Basic Neurosis.* Grune & Stratton, New York, 1949.

Bergler, Edmund. *The Revolt of the Middle-Aged Man.* Reprinted by International Universities Press, Madison, CT. 1985.

Bergler, Edmund. *The Superego.* Grune & Stratton Inc. New York, 1952. International Universities Press, Madison, CT 1989.

Bergler, Edmund. *The Writer and Psychoanalysis.* Reprinted by International Universities Press, Madison, CT. 1986.

Bettelheim, Bruno. *Freud's Vienna and Other Essays.* Vintage Books. New York.

Bloom, Sandra A. "American Health Care: They Say There's a Crisis, But a Crisis of What?" *The Journal of Psychohistory.* Vol. 21, No.3 Winter 1994. pp. 301-332.

Campbell, Joseph. *The Power of Myth*. Doubleday. New York, 1988.

Coles, Robert. *The Moral Life of Children*. The Atlantic Monthly Press, Boston. 1988.

Diagnostic and Statistical Manual of Mental Disorders, Third Edition—Revised. American Psychiatric Association. Washington, DC. 1987.

Emerson, Ralph Waldo. "Self-Reliance." *The American Tradition in Literature*. Grosset & Dunlap, 1974. pp. 648-649.

Erikson, Erik H. *Childhood and Society*. W. W. Norton and Co. New York, 1963.

Erikson, Erik H. *Insight and Responsibility*. W.W. Norton & Co. New York, 1964.

Erikson, Erik H. *The Life Cycle Completed*. W.W. Norton & Co. New York, 1982.

Fromm, Erich. *The Heart of Man: Its Genius for Good and Evil*. Harper & Row. New York, 1964.

Franklin, Benjamin. *The Autobiography. The American Tradition in Literature*. Grosset & Dunlap. 1974. p. 139.

Gay, Peter. Ed. *The Freud Reader*. W.W. Norton. New York, 1989.

Goleman, Daniel. *Emotional Intelligence: Why it can matter more than IQ*. Bantam Books. New York, 1995.

Greider, William. *Who Will Tell the People: The Betrayal of American Democracy*. Simon & Schuster. New York, 1992.

Hand, Learned. "The Spirit of Liberty." *Lend Me Your Ears: Great Speeches in History*. Ed. William Safire. W.W. Norton. New York, 1992. p. 63.

Hunt, Morton. *The Story of Psychology*. Doubleday. New York, 1993.

Jung, Carl. *The Undiscovered Self*. New American Library. New York, 1958.

Lramer, Joel; Alstad, Diana. *The Guru Papers: Masks of Authoritarian Power.* Frog, Ltd. Berkeley, CA 1993. (Distributed by North Atlantic Books.)

Lowen, Alexander. *Narcissism: Denial of the True Self.* Macmillan, New York, 1983.

Marin, Peter. *Freedom and Its Discontents.* Steerforth Press. South Royalton, Vermont, 1995.

Maslow, Abraham H. *Toward a Psychology of Being.* Van Nostrand Reinhold. New York, 1968.

Piaget, Jean. *The Moral Judgment of the Child.* The Free Press, New York, 1965.

Piaget, Jean. *Six Psychological Studies.* Vintage Books, New York, 1968.

Roheim, Geza. *Psychoanalysis and Anthropology.* International Universities Press. New York, 1950, 1973.

"Psychotherapy and Society." *The Journal of Psychohistory.* Vol. 20, No. 3. Winter 1993.

Tuchman, Barbara W. *The March of Folly: From Troy to Vietnam.* Ballantine Books. New York, 1984.

Zukav, Gary. *The Dancing Wu Li Masters. An Overview of the New Physics.* Bantam edition. New York, 1980.

Also by Peter Michaelson:

Secret Attachments: Exposing the Roots of Addictions and Compulsions
See Your Way to Self-Esteem: An In-Depth Study of the Causes and Cures of Low Self-Esteem

To read more of Mr. Michaelson's writing or to order his books, visit his web site at www.QuestForSelf.com